Your Natural Garden

Quarto.com

© 2025 Quarto Publishing Group USA Inc.
Text and Photos © 2025 Kelly D. Norris

First Published in 2025 by Cool Springs Press, an imprint of The Quarto Group,
100 Cummings Center, Suite 265-D, Beverly, MA 01915, USA.
T (978) 282-9590 F (978) 283-2742

Cool Springs Press titles are also available at discount for retail, wholesale, promotional, and bulk purchase. For details, contact the Special Sales Manager by email at specialsales@quarto.com or by mail at The Quarto Group, Attn: Special Sales Manager, 100 Cummings Center, Suite 265-D, Beverly, MA 01915, USA.

29 28 27 26 25   1 2 3 4 5

ISBN: 978-0-7603-8822-8

Digital edition published in 2025
eISBN: 978-0-7603-8823-5

Library of Congress Cataloging-in-Publication Data

Names: Norris, Kelly D., author.
Title: Your natural garden : a practical guide to caring for an ecologically vibrant home garden / by Kelly D. Norris
Other titles: Practical guide to caring for an ecologically vibrant home garden
Identifiers: LCCN 2024021510 (print) | LCCN 2024021511 (ebook) | ISBN 9780760388228 (hardcover) | ISBN 9780760388235 (ebook)
Subjects: LCSH: Organic gardening--Handbooks, manuals, etc. | Human ecology. | Handbooks and manuals. lcgft
Classification: LCC SB453.5 N67 2024 (print) | LCC SB453.5 (ebook) | DDC 635/.0484--dc23/
    eng/20240510
LC record available at https://lccn.loc.gov/2024021510
LC ebook record available at https://lccn.loc.gov/2024021511

Design: Tanya Jacobson, tanyajacobson.co
Photography: Kelly D. Norris, except where noted

Printed in China

Your Natural Garden

A Practical Guide to Caring for an Ecologically Vibrant Home Garden

By

KELLY D. NORRIS

COOL
SPRINGS
PRESS

Contents

◄ *A dry, sandy portion of Three Oaks Garden (Des Moines, Iowa, US), my home and studio, playfully called The Romp, a planting inspired by sand prairies and glades around the upper Midwest.*

This hillside meadow along a busy residential street demonstrates a new way for planting the places we call home. Planting design by Kelly Norris (West Des Moines, Iowa, US).

Introduction

What is a garden? It's an obvious question with a seemingly elusive answer. An old yarn of horticultural lore states that a garden doesn't exist without the gardener. You can feel that in your back and knees, maybe most because a garden results from the act of planting. You emplace plants where they may or may not have otherwise occurred on their own. Making a garden requires this seminal act. What happens afterward— *gardening*—can considerably influence the garden. But these activities alone, independent of emplacement, amount to nothing more than an intelligent mammal disturbing and arresting the plants of its environment. What if a garden could be second nature to our way of life, a beautiful disturbance that celebrates place and grows largely on its own energy? What if a garden wasn't just a product of human industry but a place that supported life?

People make gardens with what they have and what they know. When you know more, you do more. Whether you own land or not, gardening is an opportunity to engage the place you call home, whether collected in containers on your balcony or sprawling across the expanse of your backyard. But the place you garden isn't so easily confined to a property boundary. The place you garden is home to more than your wild imagination and the length of your watering hose.

Across the world and its cultures, humans have survived and thrived with gardens for much of our history. Gardens have been a component of human habitats, equally as likely to appear inevitable in the context of place as often as they have thrived in decadent opposition. Early Chinese characters for gardens depicted walls confining captive game and food crops. In Europe, one word for garden comes from Old English *geard*, which means fence or enclosure. We seem to have a knack for imposing order on our surroundings. Water appears in gardens throughout history, epitomized in Abrahamic religions by the paradisiacal Garden of Eden near the confluence of flowing rivers. Ancient garden sites like Sigiriya in Sri Lanka depict an elaborate architectural vision imposed on a granite promontory. Indigenous peoples across the world domesticated crops from their native landscapes, sometimes in cultivation but often by tending wild populations in an agroecological manner. Grains, legumes, and tree nuts became food. No matter the era, gardening is a method of human engagement with the natural world, a reflection of the social ecology of our species.

Against this diverse history and facing a warming world, I imagine a consilient and inclusive approach for living and growing closer to the nature of place. The gardens we inhabit don't grow in a vacuum any more than a beaver's dam or an anthill is separate from its surroundings. Every creature, based on its capabilities, creates and adapts to its environment in an act of survival. Our garden habitats can and should support bumblebees and barbecues, sawflies and soccer games. You, dear human, need the garden as much as your place, your habitat, needs you living well with it.

The book's title appeals to our relationship with the places we live, work, play, and steward. While it could reasonably imply possession, consider the prevalence of human activities across the Earth. What *isn't* yours to steward, care for, or be concerned with? What landscape doesn't deserve a more concerted relationship with its most abundant mammal? Your natural garden—our natural garden—grows well beyond anything you plant inside *your* garden gate.

Living well with a place requires a relationship, even if you're conscious about how much you invest. Phrases like "low maintenance" have infiltrated garden literature for decades and with good sense. At some point, there's a practical limit to the time and treasure any person can invest in a plot of land. But having a relationship with landscape and the life it supports doesn't immediately command more work. It does, however, warrant more attention.

I'm writing this book as a primer for cultivating an ecological garden. Amid an era of cultural inflection, many wide-eyed gardeners have found their way back to the land, wondering how to do less and achieve more. But ecological gardening isn't always about doing less. It's about understanding *why* and *how* you engage with the landscape. Gardening is an act of participation in the web of life. In some ways, it's about doing *more* for the world around you, even if the labor looks different. We need new methods and new rules for an infinite ecological game. Once you've begun borrowing inspiration from wild plant communities and creating habitats, how do you decide *what* to do in the wilder garden? How confident are you about letting plants take the lead?

This book offers a way forward, a source of gentle encouragement and honed insights. To borrow a phrase from poet Wendell Berry, I hope to cultivate your peace with wild things.

While the objective of this book is ostensibly about caring for a natural garden, it's equally about thinking of the garden as an environment in which you live. This book explores gardening as an active, positive force of ecological disturbance. In this way of thinking, the gardener becomes a keystone species or at least a proxy for one, the steward of a complex system held in orbit with knowledge and practice; weeding, planting, watering, and pruning are all gestures of order. Even the most unruly garden is an orderly place.

In my writing, I make considerable effort to avoid too many prescriptions and, where necessary, grant considerable license to dispense them. I try to avoid overgeneralization; nature is complex, even that which lives close to home. Readily prescribed solutions often arise from overgeneralizations of good but limited data.

Throughout the book, I balance context with instructions. Understanding how to do something makes it meaningful. While fundamental concepts guide ecological practices, they should inspire humility and optimism, curiosity and caution. We don't have every answer, and our errors are rarely permanent, even when we're wrong. We understand more today than we did a century ago amid our continued ecological ignorance. Further, ten gardeners will no doubt choose ten slightly different ways of executing their options as they interpret them from these pages. I reason that doing somewhat different things towards the same goal is naturally entropic.

I've organized the book around four themes. **Place** underpins our aesthetic experience with the necessary context and local vibrancy. A gardener must fundamentally understand a place and its dynamic nature for plants to thrive. **Complexity** challenges gardeners. But a biodiverse garden is inherently complex and requires learning to let plants take the lead, even as we remain a keystone to the garden's existence. Cultivating complexity follows a different playbook than traditional gardening. Intervening with complexity is required to preserve the **Legibility** of the garden. While an abundant garden brims with life, the human mind must perceive pattern, form, structure, color, rhythm, or any aesthetic dynamics we use to interpret our world. This critical interface between aesthetics and ecology paves the way toward greater cultural awareness and acceptance of natural gardens. The final section of the book asks you to be mindful of the flow of energy through the garden. **Flow** manifests through many organisms at many points in time and space. The flow of life through a nature-forward garden is the chief reason for doing it.

In writing, I feel obligated to share natural and empirical knowledge. I am uninterested in simply persuading you with information without underscoring the complexity of its origins. Turning information into knowledge requires human experience. That experience is rooted in the place you live. While I've had the pleasure of planting in many places, I'm most connected to Three Oaks, my home and studio garden, which naturally colors my views on how to approach planting and gardening with the nature of place. I write about principles, concepts, and methods, admittedly for a global audience (i.e., "wherever books are sold"). What follows in the

Growing a natural garden is an act of consilience, but the results might surprise you.
There is no one way to make a garden with place nor a singular outcome.

pages ahead likely deserves and demands variation as appropriate for your place, if it's even appropriate at all. Consider your context first and then think about how to apply the ideas accordingly. Read the book like a series of prompts: what action will you take next? I hope this book starts conversations; it's hardly the last word on anything.

I firmly believe that gardens will save the planet, even if only partly because of what we plant. As I wrote in *New Naturalism*, planting is an act of commencement and something you should commit to keep doing. But the next process—gardening—is an act of stewardship, a method for cultivating a better life.

Place

"People often talk about genius loci, or the spirit of a place, but too often, they impose their own personal preferences and patterns on a piece of land, which can alter its inherent character and obliterate the natural dialogue of the place. Of course, some areas have more to say than others."

—Louise Agee Wrinkle in *Listen to the Land*

From the outset, you must connect your gardening ambitions to some reality of place. Place is a complex phenomenon in human culture, a multifaceted way of ascribing meaning to physical space. You live in places. You recreate in places. You travel to and from places. Yet the notion of place has often eluded a gardener's thinking, enticed as we are by inspirations and plants from anywhere. What defines the place we live and work? Even if we know our address, do we know our natural neighbors?

In an ecological context, place is more than just a geographical location. Place exists in many dimensions: its present natural features reflect legacies of human disturbance while suggesting its trajectory into the future. Each version of place deserves consideration. This leads to a more compelling approach to planting and gardening, mainly as you understand indigenous plant communities, how they have changed, and how they can inspire your methods. Methods relate to context. In some contexts, some methods make sense. Every method, however, doesn't universally apply. That's why context matters. Your garden should resonate, resemble, and reveal the nature of its place.

In the end, planting and gardening should reflect the story of a place, celebrating its natural history while preempting its future. The nature of place and its legacy informs what kind of landscape is possible and what plants will thrive given those circumstances. Place is not a limiting factor but a grounding one. Place is the subject of your garden, not simply its setting. A place isn't merely bare ground for wide-open dreams, nor is it a mandate. Place is both physical and imagined, an experience that leads to deep questions. How will you make a garden *here?*

Drone photography shifts the human perspective of a garden towards the birds-eye view of a place to land, browse, or nest.

What Is a Natural Garden?

Your garden is alive. At this moment, some creature stirs in the underbrush, buzzes between flowers, and flits between branches. Go for a walk, and you might encounter a few thousand other life forms if only you could know the herds of microbes that gently squish beneath your feet. Can you name this life, calling out to it as if recognizing a friend walking down the street? Never mind the plants for a moment, although that's enough of a chore. You probably know a few charismatic birds, honeybees, a regular browsing mammal (probably unwelcomed), frogs and snakes, maybe a worm, and common butterflies if you're really paying attention. The vast majority slip by unnoticed, perhaps as indifferent to us as we are to them. Of course, gardens are not natural, or so the saying goes.

The complexity of nature inspires protective attitudes, but curiosity can lead to more abundant possibilities. Our preoccupation with labels—pristine, wild, natural, cultivated, garden—leaves significant parts of the world unattended, hiding in plain sight without acknowledgment or recognition. Many authors have hoed this row, articulating a fragile dichotomy between "wilderness" (or a thesaurus of other synonyms to suit their purposes) and "gardens" in an attempt to plainly state that one cannot be the other. The boundaries couldn't be more fluid.

It's time for a more generous definition of nature beyond the binary of what humans create and what we hike through. Whether we realize it or not, our gardens are already connected to the nature around them; little that moves pays heed to the garden gate. Though the creatures that come to call a natural garden home may not be the same cohort that calls a natural area home, that doesn't diminish their value.

Bombus griseocollis *(brown-belted bumblebee) on* Asclepias incarnata *(swamp milkweed)*

If anything, the vibrancy of their differences deserves celebration. Why undertake intellectual gymnastics to exclude gardening as something separate when the worms, wrens, and woodchucks take up residence anyway?

When we blur the dichotomies of "wild" nature and "tended" nature, we find a new role as creative, supportive, and deeply appreciative stewards of nonhuman life. We cultivate awareness of the place we grow as much as anything with actual roots. We garden by moving away from models of control to something that embraces unpredictability and constant change. A natural garden is a place of consilience. With a new mindset, the creative opportunities are boundless.

◄ *The Romp, a dry meadow at Three Oaks Garden (Des Moines, Iowa, US).*

The Infinite Game

In his 1986 book, *Finite and Infinite Games*, author James Carse wrote:

> Gardening is not outcome-oriented. A successful harvest is not the end of a gardener's existence, but only a phase of it. As any gardener knows, the vitality of a garden does not end with a harvest. It simply takes another form. Gardens do not 'die' in the winter but quietly prepare for another season.

Carse posited that in a finite game, participants play to win. Finite games refer to structured activities like sports and agronomy where participants adhere to set rules, acknowledge the limitations of the field, and declare winners and losers along the way to points or produce. Horticulture, no doubt, evolved from this agronomic tradition, adhering to the rules of a finite game.

However, an ecological garden operates in a different field of play. The rules are different. In an infinite game, participants play with the purpose of prolonging it. Infinite games shift rules, challenge boundaries, and have no use for scorecards or finality. Infinite players understand that the potential for change within a garden is amplified by its complexity, which enhances its vibrancy, something that transcends seasons. Infinite gardeners understand that plants are teammates. This subtle semantic shift can produce dramatic results while liberating gardeners from chronological expectations.

What Is Your Goal?

If the objective of a natural gardener is to stay in the game, why are you playing it? For many readers, your natural gardening journey is already underway, even if only recently. You may have started from scratch, ripping up lawn to plant a garden habitat. Maybe you're slowly steering an existing garden towards more complexity and diversity. Maybe you're finding a way to grow food for your family and increase the amount of vegetation that supports wildlife around you. Regardless of what kind of garden you have already or your horticultural aspirations, consider the question: what's your goal in living with a natural garden? Are you focused on the conservation of a single species? A group of organisms? Do you relish the idea of plant-driven landscapes even if you're still learning about other dimensions of nature? Do you seek a more ecological lifestyle? The list could run on pages with sundry motivations.

I like to think of gardens as patches in an expansive ecological quilt, a patchwork tapestry of irregular pieces and motley construction. This comparison is not just metaphorical but supported by several studies indicating a shift in our understanding of conservation. Small, interconnected habitat patches in urban areas are proving to be just as crucial for biodiversity as the vast, undisturbed expanses of nature typically found in national parks or wildlife refuges.

The nature of this quilt varies in a subtle, shifting mosaic across the living surface of the globe. If you cut it into smaller pieces, not all patches would be the same, even as they shared common species, communities, or landscape patterns. For instance, you can imagine that an urban landscape would contain different species and processes than a similarly sized rural landscape. Understanding the context of place brings natural gardening into focus: What are you trying to steward? Are those species present in your near regional landscape? How do you garden a habitat that meaningfully impacts their abundance?

While you may choose to focus on plants, many other creatures call your natural garden home. Look closely, and you'll see a pair of stilt bugs (family Berytidae).

▶

How you think about the issues helps to clarify your approach. I don't aim to persuade you with a singular, avowed method but rather to present an array of methods that work in practice. Your gardening practice becomes a dialogue you cultivate with your place. In turn, your goals likely morph with time as you understand that planting and caring for a natural garden isn't above a fixed result but rather a celebration of process, experience, and connection.

To be clear, in the footprint of a residential garden, long-term stewardship of biodiversity runs up against some challenges. The size of your garden, almost independent of your actions, defines the game before you even make your first move. Consider a densely and diversely planted garden under a half-acre (2,023.4 m²) in size. For the thousands of soil-dwelling organisms beneath your garden, you are merely a rumble on the rooftop of an expansive palatial estate. For insects, some species could live on this much land for generations. For larger mammals and many birds, a parcel of this size offers a quick stop-off on a roving lunch tour, maybe a nesting place if you're lucky, and probably only for those species who don't mind humans in their midst. Thus, your small patch presents a conundrum: what's beneficial for one group of organisms might totally disrupt the lives of others in a relatively modest space. Your priority is the integrity of the system, as measured by the abundance of fauna and thriving vegetation. By viewing our gardens as integral parts of a greater ecological system, we recognize their potential to collectively support and enhance biodiversity in significant ways. Achieving this happens through acts of stewardship.

Natural Garden Defined

A natural garden reflects and enhances the ecology of place through active and conscious disturbances in harmony with the environment. A natural garden emphasizes complementarity, observation, and holistic well-being. A natural garden grows from anthropogenic acts working conjunctively with natural processes. Our actions should keep us shoulder-to-shoulder with our natural neighbors, leading gardens to increase in ecological value over time. This active stewardship returns greater dividends than passive maintenance.

Natural gardening celebrates the uniqueness of a place by cooperating with its native flora to contribute effectively to the local ecosystem. Native species stitch the patch to the quilt. Plants are living entities that play complex roles in their ecosystems. By understanding and respecting them, we can create abundant gardens that contribute to surrounding ecosystems. A natural garden is a complex system of plants living and interacting together rather than a mere collection of individual species. To understand the lives of any species in the system requires knowing more than where they are from.

Moreover, natural gardening is akin to music, choreography, or theater, rather than static visual arts. It embraces the dimension of time, acknowledging the ever-shifting, dynamic nature of plant communities as the most visible ecological artifact. This perspective celebrates the continual transformation inherent in living landscapes.

◁ *By connecting the lives of the local flora and fauna, season to season, your garden strengthens the ecological fabric of your place. Meadow Nord, our front yard meadow here at Three Oaks Garden (Des Moines, Iowa, US).*

A Gardener Is a Keystone Species

The act of planting is uniquely human. Planting has evolved as a human behavior, first for sustenance, then for pleasure and contemplation, and now as an intentional way of engaging the environment. Ironically, when defined by acts of planting, gardens can exist without *gardening* by a human player, even if they slowly become unrecognizable as such to most other humans. Consider a neglected, historic landscape that retains some elements of its plantings, even if it exceeded reasonable horticultural standards for care and legibility. Absent gardening, this abandoned landscape develops entirely at the behest of the plants in it, yet its composition is entirely contrived. Those contrivances linger with consequences.

In ecology, a keystone species preserves the structure of an ecological community. Removing a keystone species leads to a reorganization and wholesale reordering of food chains and other macro-scale ecological processes. In the Anthropocene, humans are often characterized as "hyperkeystone" species because of the outsized footprint of our activities. We're grafted onto the land even as we've grown from it. In the not-so-distant past, large herbivores were principal keystone species in environments around the world, transporting seeds and nutrients across land as they grazed. While humanity coexisted for thousands of years with megafauna, overkill and habitat disruption in the last few hundred years have revealed the profound importance of landscape-scale herbivory on biodiversity. Rewilding organizations in Europe and conservation organizations in North America often advocate for restoring "charismatic" grazers and apex predators. While these ideas have little direct impact on home gardening, how do you, as a gardener, become a keystone species to facilitate natural functions in your small plot? How do you create an ecosystem where plants lead you to interact instead of vice versa? How do you simulate grazing megafauna?

The task is less absurd than it initially sounds, although I won't judge you for conjuring up a costume for your efforts. In later sections, I'll encourage you to perform gardening tasks like weeding with the coarseness of an animal moving steadily, systematically, and continuously across the land. Regardless of the size of your plot, you, as the gardener, become a force of disturbance, both a proxy for and a component of natural processes. Some natural processes don't have space to play out in small gardens. Your actions introduce dynamism into the landscape, a positive disruption that creates opportunities for life to flourish. This gardening is less intense and less fussy by traditional standards.

As landscapes increase in size, the scale of interventions becomes less targeted on a specific plant or area and instead focuses on whole levels of the ecosystem. Nobody pulls weeds in a 10,000-acre (4,047 hectare) forest. But managing its canopy, thinning understory, and controlling fires all have the same effect of working on many species at once. That systematic approach scales just as well to 10,000 square feet (929 m²) or less.

Your natural garden won't flourish if you're micro-managing it. Cultivating a biocentric garden requires an appreciation for the ability of other life forms to adapt to change. As a result, some plants will meet their demise at the success of others; most plants don't live forever. These garden-scale changes may happen despite your economic contributions to the system, although hopefully not catastrophically. As the British gardener and writer Christopher Lloyd famously wrote, "The great wonder in gardening is that so many plants live."

Extending this mindset beyond plants deepens the rewards. What are "pests," after all, but creatures that we don't appreciate or understand? Minimizing pesticides or mechanical tools to control "pests" in the garden is a reasonable first step. While you may find ways to favor plant growth over the appetites of overpopulated urban herbivores, you shouldn't have a warring mindset—you, the gardener, versus everything else. Ultimately, the methods favor the accumulation of life—plants to protozoa—not the elimination of some in favor of others. Doing little or nothing with a modicum of patience can reveal a deeper understanding of how organisms live in your garden environment. While challenging, try not to react to the headline without reading the whole story first.

As you think like the keystone species of recent nat-ural history, keep the focus on tasks that, when done today, have implications tomorrow and beyond. Start small and develop a practice that fits the scale of your property. As you gain confidence about planting and stewarding, you may recognize opportunities in your landscape for engaging other strategies and ideas. Even with similar methods, these projects carried out in different years will have different results. Together, these interventions become another stitch that connects your patch in time and space to the bigger quilt. The most daunting and yet liberating idea to keep in your mind as you kneel to the ground is that your garden transforms slowly and unceasingly. It's constantly dynamic.

Keep rambunctious species—like Ranunculus acris *(meadow buttercup)—in check by mimicking its natural control: grazing.*

As you undertake natural plantings, you may ponder if you're naturalizing your garden or gardening with nature. Planting design by Kelly Norris, Three Oaks Garden (Des Moines, Iowa, US).

21

What Does Wild Mean?

What does wild mean to you? If you opened a dictionary, you might find words like "uncultivated," "untamed," or "natural environment," all with a whiff of romantic suggestion: humans weren't involved. The origins of the word would seem to imply some otherness beyond whatever the viewer considers civilized, developed, tamed, or controlled. There are, of course, significant problems with attempting to categorize the world like this, not the least of which is the fact that *wildness* is largely a narrative of our own devising.

The problem with wildness is that it attempts to separate humanity from the whole of nature. In what period in the last 100,000 years have the landscapes of the world lacked human footprints? Historically, what some people perceived as wild landscapes were, in fact, a result of agroecological practices implemented by Indigenous communities. The notion of wildness arose as a misinterpretation of how humans inhabit landscapes.

Absent those indigenous lifestyles, biomes lack key players that shaped their character and identity for thousands of years, even where many other organisms still exist. In their place, humans today interact in vastly different ways with these landscapes, leading to the widespread ecological disruption that's characteristic of modern times. National parks, forests, and reserves are monuments to untrammeled natural history, separated from the most intense human activity; long may they thrive. Back inside the envelope of human disturbance, armed with advanced technology and new ideas, we might harness the folly of recent history and sow seeds for a more verdant future. Your natural garden is one such seed.

The word *wild* in modern usage, at least as it relates to gardening, conveys a hodgepodge of meanings. You may begin thinking that you want to give up control, in deference to the ways plants live with a place as they find it. **Rewilding**, as the approach is known, gives ecological processes time and space to evolve, even when the results look different than recent natural precedents.

Restoration, alternately, attempts to conserve a previous state of nature as the best-case scenario. If focused on "restoration," you will think differently about plant selection, plant communities, and stewardship than a gardener focused on "rewilding." You likely desire to cultivate a habitat for specific groups of organisms like pollinators and birds.

You may adopt either of these mindsets in your home landscape. Each will produce gardens that look and function differently, while still supporting a greater amount of life than the prototypical front yard. In either respect, you'll challenge cultural norms about what gardens look like and can be. But is it wild?

The trick question is "Does this look wild to you?" In reality, this meadow has sprung to life in just a few decades after the cessation of mining and logging activities along this Colorado mountain road.

23

Integrating outdoor living spaces with ecological plantings offers intimate opportunities to observe and celebrate the nature of place.

Defining Home Ground

Places for planting necessitate different rules. Context matters, so consider the nature beyond your patch. Where you garden—in the city, its suburbs, or in a rural landscape—has a dramatic influence on the nature of your garden. Most humans reside in urban areas, which, by most estimates, account for about 3 percent of the world's land area. That number is on track to double by 2060, at which point nearly 70 percent of the global population will reside in urban areas. This is our habitat. Most gardens and managed landscapes are small and privately held inside this envelope of human activities. In some cities around the world, gardens account for more than 25 percent of urban land, even as urbanization displaces natural habitats and traditional croplands. Although this land has been disturbed by development, turned over, and tilled under as cities grow, it presents opportunities for individuals to produce cultural change collectively. The nature of cities hinges on homeowners' attitudes, motivations, and practices.

Embrace Your Place

No doubt, as you begin gardening, you've taken stock of the features that make your place *your place*. How does your ongoing planting and gardening magnify these features? What we perceive determines how we act.

Natural gardens come in many forms and come to life through various methods. Regardless, there are three phases to any garden's evolution and development: design and conception, establishment, and persistence. The least disruptive modes—minimal tillage, establishing communities from seed, and embracing existing vegetation—often yield a faster return of natural processes and systems. But those methods aren't uniformly applicable to every site or place. Of course, if you invest in large plants from the outset, you shoulder a

You can integrate food production with ecological approaches, provided enhanced soil fertility doesn't favor overly competitive plants.

significant establishment burden. While larger plants often produce satisfying short-term results, they only do so when followed by significant investments in the establishment period and don't always guarantee long-term success.

Every act of gardening that stewards your place also strengthens your attachment to it. Creating experiences for you, your family, or even your friends and neighbors plays a role in the social ecology of our species. It forges connections with the environment and its atmosphere. The more you do it, the more you can't live without it. Most experienced gardeners could attest to this, but connecting those communal activities to a place only deepens the likelihood that you'll identify with the work and its rewards.

Organic Versus Ecological Gardening

In your natural garden, you may adopt organic and ecological gardening strategies to achieve your goals. But the approaches deserve some analysis, which may help you understand your current garden if you've engaged with any of these practices. Both approaches share common goals but differ in how they achieve them.

Organic gardening rigorously avoids synthetic chemicals, a tenet shared with ecological gardening, but focuses on building healthy soil through composting and using organic fertilizers, which is where a critical distinction emerges. While organic gardening seeks to enhance soil fertility through nonchemical methods, ecological gardening mimics natural systems and processes. Ecological gardening deemphasizes fertility and productivity as a benchmark for garden performance. In your natural

garden, you should focus on conserving the soil by minimizing soil degradation and erosion, promoting and facilitating biodiversity that benefits plants best adapted to those conditions.

Organic gardening often confronts plant pests with a rapid-response mindset, adopting methods like biological control, physical removal, organic sprays, or plant selection that actively discourage or eradicate them from the garden environment. A more ecological approach considers the organism, its life cycle, and its relative impact on the garden. Does it have a natural predator? Does it occur seasonally or for only a limited time? Asking questions first leads to a decision-tree mentality: you may not need to do anything. If something isn't eating plants in your natural garden, how much is it participating in the ecosystem?

Becoming a Natural Gardener

Initially, you may follow the playbook closely, sticking to prescribed planting recommendations and known methods. This cautious but sincere approach may cause you to question novel ideas and techniques. You'd settle for small gains, knowing you hadn't risked too much in achieving them. Your efforts are targeted, focused, and likely to balance the many uses and purposes of the residential landscape you call home.

As you experience more, you may question the foundations of your initial approach, reaching for new experimental methods. You begin to embrace the novelty of the garden ecosystem, even as you remain focused on how it connects and interacts with the extensional landscape. Your lifestyle grows to match the garden environment, celebrating the interface between your activities and nature. Your metrics will grow as much as your garden.

The uncertain and dynamic nature of ecological knowledge raises questions about how to protect the environment. Why, much less how, should we act when we seemingly know so little? Despite the lack of consensus, the precautionary principle inspires preventative action to foster local ecology. You may not believe you can change the world, but you can plant your corner of it into a beautiful, vibrant place for life as you know it.

In any case, don't let your enthusiasm run off with reality. Starting small is always advisable, particularly for the first season or three after committing to a new planting. These initial years of establishment, often infused with patience and diligence, reveal much about the nature of your place. Once you see through the establishment cycle, you can size up your ambitions with what you've learned about the place. Further, with time and experience, you'll gain the confidence to make tougher decisions, like when to remove certain weedy species from your garden or how to remove a dying tree while preserving its cycle of decay for the benefit of the garden ecosystem. All of this work hones your relationship with place.

Purpose-driven gardening emerged as a palpable trend in the mid-2000s alongside the widespread use of social media. While the modern internet gives us an expansive view of the world, the algorithms that power those platforms also heavily curate our views. On the upside, you can immerse yourself in communities that foster and cultivate your interests. The downside is a nearly constant effort to verify the information exchanged on those platforms as empirical or supported by broad experience. You will gain confidence and knowledge as you develop a stewardship mindset through practice. Often, knowing a single answer isn't nearly as important as asking several good questions.

Don't underestimate your ability to plant your lively corner of the world into a beautiful, more vibrant place. ▶

Places for Planting

The panacea of traditional gardening rests on the assumption that a gardener can manipulate the environment to their will. It's difficult for most gardeners to even imagine how to commence a new planting without first undoing the vegetation that already exists. In his essay "The Nature Garden," early twentieth-century landscape architect Warren Manning wrote:

> I would have you give your thoughts to a new type of gardening wherein the Landscaper recognizes, first, the beauty of existing conditions and develops this beauty to the minutest detail by the elimination of material that is out of place in a development scheme by selective thinning, grubbing, and trimming, instead of by destroying all natural ground cover vegetation or modifying the contour, character, and water context of existing soil.

His ideas were as antithetical then as unheard of now.

Manning worked throughout his 20s for Frederick Law Olmsted before opening his own practice. Over nearly half a century, he contributed to or led the design of over 1,700 projects, many of which were public spaces. He was a champion of the "wild garden" concept, in his words, but with a distinct emphasis on site specificity, a view that set his approach apart from the natural aesthetic approach emerging in Europe at the time. He valued uncovering, revealing, and celebrating the unique character and inherent beauty of the place. His early works revealed a fascination with local plant life, which he sought to amplify by removing elements of the site that suppressed their beauty or functional qualities. As scholar Robin Karson put it, "Art, for Manning, was not separate from the natural system, but rather an expression of it." His work underscores the artfulness of naturalistic gardening, no less than any prior form of ornamental horticulture, and its power to transform our surroundings through the medium of plant growth.

Manipulating Place

At some point in the life of most gardens, you will need to undertake some earthwork to shape the form or function of a space. If you live in a newly constructed home or neighborhood, these opportunities define the making of your natural garden from the outset. When new homes are built, take advantage of the opportunity to replant vegetation in the disturbed area. Rectify disturbance with purposeful planting.

You should do as much to understand your topography before you begin to manipulate place. The slope of your site and the flow of surface water define most projects, either to retain soil for construction or to shape the path of water to reduce its erosive potential. You could imagine any number of earthworks and hardscapes to accomplish your goal, varying from bunds and swales to fully-fledged walls and permanent water features. If you live in an area prone to sudden precipitation events, you may devise a series of so-called "rain gardens" to divert water away from engineered infrastructure like storm drains or culverts into areas where it percolates slowly into the ground. A proper assessment of water flow and movement is crucial before investing in large plantings. Plants play a consequential role after construction but need a fair chance to grow into the job.

More than 100 Betula populifolia *(gray birch) form a uniquely original allée at Stan Hywet Hall &*
Gardens (Akron, Ohio, US). Landscape architecture by Warren Manning.

Dozens of books exist to guide your efforts in constructing an array of landscape and habitat features, from bioswales and rain gardens to walls and patios. My only counsel is to consider how these spaces can support all forms of life. Build them sensitively. Use repurposed materials when possible. Soften the joints of hardscapes with living vegetation that cools the surface. Embrace the hardscape walls as nesting cavities for wasps and bees, even reptiles. Welcome the frogs and dragonflies that frequent your water feature. See every intervention as having multiple outcomes. At a minimum, these landscape features become viewing platforms for the living garden.

Site Preparation

A new planting involves some disturbance. Your goal is to minimize the magnitude of disturbance as much as possible and maximize the environmental response. No method of site preparation is without consequence. For instance, tillage disturbs microbial and microorganismal networks while reaggregating soil structure and removing habitat options for ground-nesting organisms. Smothering existing vegetation disrupts soil gas exchanges and kills off whole ecosystems of microbes close to the surface. Herbicides used to kill existing vegetation can persist in soil organic matter, depending on the chemical used, and have short-term consequences for organisms living close to the surface. Each method, whether chemical or physical, interacts differently with the existing ecosystem but poses some threat to its constituents. In the long view, these disturbances are often temporary and reversible.

Whatever method you select, the goal is to transition from a state of ecological simplicity, such as a monoculture lawn, to one of rich diversity and density. Choosing the method of site preparation involves weighing the immediate effects against the long-term ecological gains. The key is understanding and respecting the unique nature of each site, tailoring the approach to optimize conditions that support more life. The accrual of biomass and the diversity of life supported by the new plantings should outweigh the initial impacts of site preparation.

In recent decades, pioneered by horticultural thinkers like Beth Chatto (UK), Cassian Schmidt (Germany), Peter Korn (Sweden), and Roy Diblik (US), the notion of leveraging lean, low-nutrient soils for establishing plantings has gained prominence. Gravel gardens are planted in deep aggregates that serve doubly as a medium for planting and also a mulch, forming a formidable layer over the soil that prevents weed seeds from germinating from either above or below. Lean soils stress plants out, but for those species that can adapt, the net result is diverse, dense vegetation with comparatively few gardening inputs. If you garden with lean soils already, this mode of planting offers a site-specific method with notable efficiencies: use less water and spend less time weeding. In urban environments defined entirely by construction and engineered soil horizons, this method yields predictable results that scale functionally and aesthetically with architectural surroundings.

When rehabbing an old garden, consider how disturbance can help achieve your goals. Removing overgrown plantings makes way for new additions and can improve legibility. Overturning the soil might also introduce new weed species or resuscitate old ones. It will almost certainly result in losses to the soil microbiota, particularly if the soil is tilled extensively. Biodiversity might wobble in the short term after a disturbance, but increased plant diversity provides more habitat and resources in the long run. Understanding the nature of site manipulation requires a 360-degree perspective relative to your objective. What do you intend to accomplish as a result of your actions?

A freshly planted prairie garden illustrating optimal, dense spacing of small plants. Initial density is an asset, even if the species composition shifts with time.

Places Change Through Acts of Gardening

As your landscape evolves in the context of place, the place will change, hopefully for the better. Your natural garden may begin as an exposed, open site in a clearing surrounded by new homes, but will grow to support more plant diversity, denser canopies, more life, and connections with the natural world. As vegetation establishes, water moves through the landscape differently, reducing your inputs as you continue planting. Wherever you start and however you see the landscape now, these shifts in composition track with the succession of plant communities, a concept explored more deeply in Section 4: Flow. Traditional gardening often seeks to arrest succession, preserving the vision of a landscape's design in static form. While possible, the resource consumption required for such stasis is antithetical to resilience. Natural gardening stands on a paradox: how much do you let a place grow before interrupting it with an act of disturbance?

As you garden with place, wisdom and knowledge accumulate from your intimate experience with land. Where does the snow melt first? Where does it linger? Which part of the garden always shows signs of the first frost? Which parts of the garden are the windiest? Do large trees create drought zones beneath their canopy? Where are the animal trails in your garden? These and 100 more questions generate rich data about your experience with the place. With any luck, the assessments you made during your initial planning proved accurate. But if not, what have you learned since that you can use to steer the garden's evolution? Don't fight intuition or observation. Understanding the nature of a place shouldn't be rife with antagonism, which only leads to exhausting more resources and mental fatigue.

As your natural garden develops, you may develop an interest in constructing habitats inspired by the wildlife surrounding you. A cottage industry exists to support these endeavors, selling everything from bug hotels to birdhouses. While quaint and useful, many of these functions will develop over time with complex vegetation. Layered living vegetation provides numerous niche opportunities for foraging, breeding, and nesting, and as vegetation dies or decays, even more nooks and crannies arise for creatures who live closer to the soil. As a short-term, initial offering, you can't go wrong with a bird feeder. But planting things that naturally feed birds with their seeds and leaving them to stand for the winter makes more sense in the long run.

The remnants of a large stump become a new habitat for ferns and understory denizens of the Pacific Northwest as seen here at Heronswood (Kingston, Washington, US) and untold creatures lurking about beneath them.

What About the Lawn You Kept?

Let's get this topic out in the open: the turfgrass covering your lawn is not guilty of a global crime. But your relationship with it may be, particularly if you have plenty of it. Why do we need so much lawn, the largest irrigated crop in North America (which feeds precious few things compared to crops raised agronomically)? Lawns are nothing more than a human proxy for a heavily grazed natural grassland. We've just taken the precedent to unnatural extremes.

Most natural gardens still feature some lawn, which, beyond its obvious applications for humans, does constitute habitat for some creatures. Ecologically managing a lawn involves adopting practices that support biodiversity, conserve resources, and minimize environmental impact while maintaining an aesthetically pleasing and functional outdoor space. As you integrate your lifestyle with the nature of a place, consider how your lawn fits into the bigger picture.

- **Reduce the size of your lawn**. Keep only as much as you need and live well with what you keep.

- **Eliminate chemical inputs.** If greenness is important, opt for organic amendments like compost to improve soil health. Don't sweat a few weeds or interlopers—an arbitrary standard of perfection doesn't apply.

- **Choose turf species that require less attention.** Select low-growing grass species or ground-covering plants that require fewer inputs, particularly mowing and irrigation. More and more alternatives to traditional turfgrass species continue to enter the market. Explore the possibilities for different aesthetics and care regimens.

- **Mow responsibly.** Mowing isn't a hobby. Mow less frequently and raise the height of your mower to promote deep root growth. Leaving grass clippings on the lawn can promote a site-specific nutrient cycle and improve soil organic matter.

Reduce lawn area and consider replacing with turfgrass alternatives like Carex spp. *(sedges) that require one or a few annual mowings.*

Even in the most extreme circumstances, like the Mojave Desert, soils support incredible biodiversity. Pictured is Abronia villosa *(desert sand verbena).*

Living Soil

Soil deserves more attention than it already gets. Research published in the *Proceedings of the National Academy of Sciences of the United States of America* (2023) estimated that soil is likely home to 59 percent of life, including everything from microbes to mammals, making it the singular most biodiverse habitat on Earth. It's also disappearing at an alarming rate. In America's agricultural heartland, 57.6 billion metric tons of topsoil have eroded since the prairie sod was broken in the middle nineteenth century. That erosion rate is double what most scientists and the U.S. Department of Agriculture deem sustainable. The loss of topsoil across the globe is an urgent and ongoing ecological crisis.

Recovering topsoil is not a quick fix, but rather a centuries-long process. In some parts of the world, an inch (2.5 cm) of topsoil forms every 1,000 years. Depending on the glacial history of your region, your garden could be growing in soils up to 10,000 years old or more. In most urban areas, though, soils are mixed or disturbed assemblages from imported and native sources. Road graders and bulldozers are the glaciers of the Anthropocene, scraping away both the life and identity of a place.

I've long struggled with the inherent assumption nested within many gardening books about what constitutes ideal garden soil. This thinking stems from an agronomic persuasion, which adopts a mindset of scarcity en route to maximizing yields. As the logic goes: better soil, better crops. In an ecological context, soils exist as a dimension of place and define the plant life that thrives there. Altering any aspect of a place isolates it from its circumstances, if even briefly, especially when soils undergo significant structural disturbance.

An Ecological View of Soil

Most gardeners understand that soils have mineral and organic components, including solids, liquids, and gases. The mineral composition of soil determines its texture, structure, and porosity. These influence key soil processes like water and air movement, root penetration, and nutrient availability. The minerals in soil tell us a lot about the underlying geology of places and how landscapes have shifted and formed through different climactic regimes. Taken together, the physical properties of soil strongly influence the mobility and retention of water and nutrients.

The biological components of soil influence its productivity. Plants make a steady supply of organic material, exuding substances from their roots that promote bacteria and fungi. As these and other microorganisms live and die, they create more organic material. Roots of perennial species also senesce seasonally, particularly in temperate climates as plants prepare for winter, leaving carbon-based structures to decompose slowly back into the soil. Organic matter also arrives from the surface, accumulating throughout the growing season as plants shed leaves, flower, senesce, and decay. In just about every earthly environment, plants materially participate in ecosystem services simply by living.

The voids between the mineral and organic components, space often filled with air and water, define the various soils of our gardening experience. These pores become channels for roots and water as well as conduits for biological activities. Larger pores promote fluidity, while smaller pores restrict it. For example, clay soils fail to percolate because clay particles are extremely small and tightly packed together, leading to smaller pore spaces in the soil that don't allow water to move through them quickly. Conversely, sandy soils are composed of larger, coarser, and loosely arranged particles, leaving plenty of room for movement. In the middle of the spectrum, loam features an aggregation of various particles and, thus, various pore sizes. It holds enough water while letting it drain uninhibited by soil structure. For this reason, most gardeners with an agronomic mindset desire loam, finding virtue in crumbly, freshly tilled soils.

Minerals, carbon, and empty space interact to support life in soil, a complex system still not fully understood by science. What we do know suggests that the vibrancy of soils isn't improved by tillage. Soils develop texture in response to the environment. The interdependent relationship between plants and soils leads to a constant exchange of energy and shifting forms. Water percolates and evaporates. Nutrients accumulate and get consumed. Some organisms disturb structure and some repair it.

Mechanical intervention brings this subterranean dance party to a screeching halt. Tillage disrupts the vertical tessellation of pores through the soil column, introducing more oxygen than required by the organisms living there. While aeration is important, especially in already compacted situations, tillage can oxygenate soils past a beneficial threshold. Mycorrhizal fungi become unflatteringly disentangled if they survive at all. Nematodes die in the churn. The addition of chemicals and fertilizers leaching into soils directly or through plants destabilizes, damages, or even destroys the nature of the system. Somebody ordered shots that nobody wanted to drink.

Planting Improves Soil

The agronomic need to do something about soil is hard to let go of. The quickest way to positively impact your soil is to plant something. The communities of organisms in the soil thrive when plant roots join the party. Increasing plant diversity boosts the diversity and abundance of soil-borne fauna, which directly affects almost all other biological properties of the soil. The more life that lives in the soil, the more life it can support.

You should understand where you begin—some soils benefit from the addition of organic matter, such as compost, biochar, and manures, especially at the outset of a new planting. These materials break down slowly, providing a steady drip of nutrients while improving soil structure and microbial communities. However, the impact of any one of these varies with soil type and application method, highlighting the importance of a tailored approach to your place.

If you have an existing garden, the soil is likely rich enough already. Traditional gardens, particularly those with a history of food crops, often boast soils with unnecessary levels of fertility, artificially enhanced by soil amendments, fertilizer, and routine composting. Research conducted in Oregon (2022) found that urban gardeners often enhanced fertility in excess, leading to soils with organic matter content well above typical agricultural recommendations. Excessive organic matter can lead to elevated levels of phosphorus and potassium, which can then be lost to local watersheds via runoff. The study found that the average organic matter in urban garden soils was double the highest typical recommendation, pointing to an overreliance on organic matter for fertilization. Organic matter is crucial for soil fertility, but excessive inputs don't always translate to increased harvests.

Most of these activities fade in importance over time in an ecological context. Plant biomass produced annually provides a slow release of organic matter, as needed, into the soil that can facilitate plant community development and establishment. In some archetypes or some regions, this accumulation of organic matter may be undesirable or limited in its efficacy. In arid climates, a huge buildup or influx of organic matter may kill many desirable species otherwise unadapted to it. In lush climates, many species might need such conditions to flourish. It all depends on the nature of the place.

If you start with degraded soil abused by human activities, cover crops offer an effective strategy for fostering ecology in advance of extensive planting. The use of cover crops dates back to ancient civilizations. In temperate regions, cover crops are often sown in fall to capture winter nutrients, while in tropical areas, they replenish soil during the hot, dry season. Species with ruderal habits and annual life cycles measure up to the task. Legumes, in particular, enhance soil organic matter and facilitate microbial communities. Some farmers are already using these methods, but there is potential for wider adoption in ecological landscaping. You get the most from cover cropping when you incorporate the organic matter produced by those species back into the soil after the growing season.

Planting helps to revitalize the soil by introducing roots into a dynamic rhizosphere.

The Garden Underground

One of the most important lessons I have learned in gardening is that the success of plantings can be affected by past human activities. These legacies, shaped not only by previous land use like farming and construction but also by soil chemistry, linger for decades or longer. Rather than stifling your gardening ambitions, understanding and adapting to these realities is key to unlocking the full potential of your site. When I came to live at Three Oaks, I encountered hardpan clay soil that confounded my ambitions, the first step in learning how to garden cooperatively with place. I underestimated its severity, tilled the ground for my first planting project, and soon realized in horror that I had worsened an already challenging situation. While gardening on heavy clay has its benefits during an extended drought, the long-term stress of compaction takes a toll on plants. While that meadow has since grown with verve, I occasionally wonder about alternative outcomes had I simply arrested the development of the lawn and planted into the remains. Would plants have established more quickly? Would I have avoided killing off some that simply drowned as water puddled at the surface when I irrigated?

As you cultivate an awareness about soil, it's easy to imagine your landscape as the sum of two gardens—one aboveground and the other below. From an ecologist's view, the environment just below ground and replete with the majority of plant root mass constitutes the rhizosphere, a dynamic interface between plants and soil. It's home to dense and diverse communities of microorganisms, including bacteria, fungi, nematodes, protozoa, and viruses. There are more microbes in a teaspoon of soil than there are people on Earth, representing anywhere from 10,000 to 50,000 species of microbes. In total, the rhizosphere plays a vital role in plant health, facilitating stress tolerance and disease resistance and enhancing overall productivity. With intensive soil interactions comes disruption and loss of soil biodiversity. As you think about taking a less intensive approach to the garden aboveground, adopt the same mindset for the garden underground.

Examining root structures gives clues for how plants live underground.

How to Know a Plant

Understanding a plant goes beyond aesthetics; it requires understanding its dynamic role in your natural garden. Most gardeners learn about plants like they would speed date, asking a few questions and taking a few answers to decide whether they should grow it. What if we approached learning about plants with a deeper curiosity about how they live? In your garden, you might describe a plant's roving, competitive habit as something natural without first considering what role, if any, you played in providing it with a rich and fertile environment to thrive. Connecting natural cues with human disturbance helps us live and garden knowledgeably in the context of place.

Knowing a plant and how to interact and care for it requires more than an origin story, even if it starts there. Ask yourself:

- What is the plant up to in its wild community or your garden? What is its role in the community, and why would you plant it?

- How long does it live, and how is it organized in the landscape?

- Is it a keystone species that supports a multitude of other creatures?

- Is it unique to a specific condition or niche? Is it a generalist with broad adaptations to a wide variety of environments?

- How does it grow? What does its architecture and habit suggest about its life cycle? When does it begin and end its growth?

- When does it flower and set seed?

Invariably, these questions require new sources of information beyond those that might simply state "full sun, well-drained soil" as a description of the circumstances in which to grow a plant. Traditional gardening emphasizes soil and light as the most essential biological prerequisites. Similarly, my driver's license says I have brown hair and live at a specific address, but what does that describe about how I live my life?

Too often, traditional gardening prioritizes the health of individual plants over the system of plants working together in a community; every plant is treated like a prized specimen. Your natural garden operates at a different speed, using a population of plants as the least common denominator for whether the garden is in sync. Individual plants are prioritized so much as they impact the bigger picture.

Further, the most consequential planting decisions persist in the landscape beyond one or a few seasons. The longest-lived plants, especially trees and shrubs, stand to contribute enormously more ecosystem services over their lifetimes than something that only lives for a season or two. Conversely, short-lived species, especially those that don't persist readily in the seed bank, pose little threat even when not indigenous to your place. A census of floristics compiled over 100 years might find that many species have appeared briefly, only to fail to persist beyond a generation or two. The history of railroads and shipyards offers a window into this phenomenon; some newcomers stick around, but most don't persist. Further, anyone who has kept up with a historic ornamental garden or attempted as much knows that most herbaceous species grown in gardens don't persist perennially for more than a decade, waxing, waning, and ultimately fading parallel to cycles of active gardening. If traditional gardening sounds like life support, is it any surprise that plants perish when you pull the plug?

You'll learn the most about a plant by growing it. Raising plants from seed—like this curious California native annual Streptanthus farnsworthianus *(Farnsworth's jewelflower)—gives you a front-row seat to its genesis and development.*

The Origin Story

Whether you've gardened for a few seasons or most of your life, you've undoubtedly encountered the ongoing debate about where plants come from. It preoccupies a lot of gardening attention, and for good reason, provided it influences ecologically valuable outcomes. Little heard in this debate is what these plants do, as if a creature's life was solely defined by its state of origin (something most readers would object to). Further, much of what we know about plants horticulturally comes from observational knowledge. Comparative trials done in industry or educational settings offer a glimpse at how plants measure up to each other but often don't reflect the plasticity of plant performance when compared to its wild origins. Conversely, sometimes data from cultivation surprises us—plants grow in gardens in entirely different ways than in their natural haunts. While an origin story offers tremendous insights into how a plant grows where it's from, it's not predictive of every situation. It's a cautionary, if not introductory, tale.

Defining nativeness is challenging and contentious, leading to debates about how to identify a species' true origin independent of any human influence. Despite the variance, it's clear that plant origin significantly impacts biodiversity. Even in disturbed urban environments, plants classified as "native" under various definitions often support higher biodiversity than non-native plants. This suggests that the boundary scale used to define native species is more crucial than the type of boundary.

Throughout the book, I'll make a concerted effort to remove emotion from the vocabulary surrounding plant origins, as unpopular as that may render the work. Words like exotic, alien, and even invasive append subjective and superficial human judgments to the life histories of plants. Of course, even using the terms "native" and "non-native" requires context. Native to where and when? Unless you live in the same region as I do, my list of native plants will arguably look different than yours, though if we live on the same continent, we probably will find considerable overlap. Imagine my humor when, as an author, I read a review of *New Naturalism* from a reader in another part of the world who expressed disappointment that I didn't recommend any "native" plants. Place is so obvious yet easily omitted as necessary context for understanding ecological concepts.

An ecological gardener should be most interested in how plants participate in and contribute to their ecosystems. How you care for or relate to a plant has little to do with where it's from but everything to do with what it is and how it grows. Adding to the confusion, many people believe native plants are "low maintenance." Should we extrapolate that the origins of a plant define how it will grow in a garden? Many gardeners have discovered the opposite. A roster of plants chosen randomly for their "nativeness" and dropped into the garden together might look more like a boxing match than a thoughtful planting (scrapes and bruises included). While local adaptation has merits, adapting to a place says nothing about *how* a plant adapts.

Consider *Rhus typhina* (staghorn sumac), a native shrub throughout eastern North America. As an early colonizer after disturbance, it forms extensive thickets that shade out the understory and exclude all but the most shade-tolerant perennials. Its flowers offer rich nectar rewards to varied swarms of bees, flies, wasps, and beetles. Its fruits feed countless bird species and small mammals, not to mention providing ample shelter for foraging and nesting activities. While manageable, staghorn sumac can quickly exceed the proportions of a residential landscape. Reading "native" on its label at the garden center is almost as subjective and meaningless as reading "ornamental" on another if the goal is to effect a behavioral change in the gardener along with an ecological shift in the landscape.

While the geographical origin of a plant species provides valuable insights, it is insufficient as the sole factor guiding plant choice in modern landscapes. Focusing exclusively on origins reduces the value of plant life in present and future terms to merely an argument over a passport stamp. There's more to the story. If you're gardening for the long game, a native plant's fitness to the realities of your landscape should warrant as much consideration as its ecological merits. A deeper and more compassionate understanding of the world as it is, despite its past failings, produces a richer view of the lives of plants. Natural gardeners have much to wrestle with, a good struggle to grow a verdant, resilient future.

Fall color on Rhus typhina *(staghorn sumac) at SummerHome Garden, an ecologically driven community garden in Denver, Colorado, US.*

Gardening in a green shade, in whatever form it comes, makes sense in an ever-warming world.

Gardening in a Warmer World

Extinctions, biodiversity loss, climate change, and environmental destruction cast a long shadow over many aspects of modern life. It's hard to ignore the plight of the planet as told by looming, sensational headlines. While the future is always unknown, there's something nearly certain about the decades ahead: the planet will warm beyond anything modern human civilization has experienced. As a result, gardens will also be different in many ways, as will your gardening, perhaps even the timing of your chores and activities. Erratic is in; consistency is out.

Trends in global warming have already shifted the nature of the places we garden. Some places already bear little resemblance to recent natural history. While you can undoubtedly create designed plant communities utilizing native species in your garden, you can't re-create the climate and the atmospheric carbon dioxide concentrations these species experienced even just 250 years ago. Overall, species are resilient, and populations adapt and survive, but not universally or equally. Change and novelty are nature's norms. We ought to remain open to the challenge of what we don't know. Here are four themes you can adopt as you square your natural garden with the uncertainty of constant environmental change.

Maximize Density and Diversity

One of the book's primary themes is to plant diversely and densely to cover as much land in vegetation as possible. This exercise has finer points, but more is more at the scale of landscape change. Maximizing verdant surface area amounts to sound risk management. A dense and diversely planted garden is more resilient to fluctuation, just like a good investment portfolio. More plants are also more effective than mulch, an oft-bandied piece of advice by many well-meaning horticulturists. While mulch has short-term value during the establishment period, it's unnecessary for an otherwise resilient garden.

Plant Carbon Sequestering Plants

You may read this as "plant more trees." Woody plants sequester carbon in timebound structures in their crowns, limbs, and trunks. In a warmer world, human environments demand comfortable microclimates shaded by urban-adapted trees that can cool modern cities' hard, reflective, and unabsorptive surfaces. But trees aren't the only plants that sequester carbon, nor do they offer a one-size-fits-all approach. Deep-rooted perennial grasses, like *Panicum virgatum* (switchgrass) and other species of historic grasslands, are living carbon sponges with roots stretching to 30 feet (9 m) deep below the surface. They sequester carbon in soil through root exudates and the seasonal decay of root litter.

Reduce Hard, Heat-Reflecting Surfaces When Possible

Paths and hardscapes are necessary for creating livable garden environments. When you consider how to build them, choose permeable materials that can become living surfaces. Natural patinas like plants and mosses soften the ground plane while preserving functionality and slowing runoff.

Be Mindful of Consumption

Home gardening can contribute to a sizable carbon footprint from horticultural plastics to hardscapes. If constructing a hardscape, stick to local building materials. This not only reduces the transportation footprint but supports local economies and vernacular aesthetics. Your garden should look like where you live. Also, reduce your reliance on peat-based potting media whenever possible; it's a finite resource. Many new alternatives utilizing compost or other repurposed brown waste, like nut hulls, continue to increase in retail availability. They often hold water and nutrients differently than traditional peat-based, soilless potting media, which requires getting used to. But the results are comparable, mainly if you're not growing plants in soilless media for more than one growing season. If planting sites require amendment, use compost or quickly decomposing materials that increase topsoil volume.

What Is Resilience?

Early in my career as a curator at a botanical garden, I became the steward of a historically significant bonsai collection that admittedly was in disrepair. I resented the task at first. Weren't these just trees in pots on life support? The moment I contemplated that irony in the frame of a traditional garden—an exercise in gardener-driven life support—was eye-opening. Similar to a conventional garden, a single bonsai is ultimately entirely sustainable with the right resources. But it's hardly what anyone would consider a resilient, low-input, self-perpetuating entity. They exist as the ultimate horticultural objective, preserved as a lifeform in a fixed amount of space, with all consequences of that environment shouldered by the caretaker and the resources they provide.

I'm partial to defining resilience in planted systems as the stability of individual plant populations and overall species diversity over an extended period, even under prolonged environmental stress. A resilient plant community keeps throttling onward amid chaos and uncertainty. It doesn't collapse or suffer a threat to its integrity. A resilient plant community adapts to the perturbance, even if its shape shifts.

Resilience challenges many assumptions about traditional gardening. What does care look like when you expect the garden to adapt and evolve? Lawns are a curious case study here. Think about the millions of gallons of water used annually to facilitate the greenness of residential turf: acts of care and conformity. Why is the consumption of resources seen as care?

Consider how you navigate the tradeoffs between resilience and care through a series of if/then statements. In the simplest example, consider a new planting. If you got lucky and it rained for several days just as you finished, you probably do not need to water quite as much until you notice the top few inches (8 to 10 cm) of the soil drying out again. But if you planted and watered a new garden in the fall and the following spring entered a drought, you might ask the question: If it's going to be this dry, do I need to water? This question propagates more questions. Are these plants "established," and if not, when is the establishment period over? At what point is the investment in establishment outweighed by the growth it generated? Would the

In a warmer, urban, densely populated world, how do landscapes in the places we live become more resilient?
Planting design by Nigel Dunnett, Barbican Centre (London, UK).

whole planting die within days if you didn't water, or could you trust that plants have some reserves to weather through it? These questions help an ecological gardener chart a path toward action and ultimately arrive at some measurement of resilience, if even by trial and error.

Every plant requires something of its environment to exist. Plants rarely need more of your dutiful fussing. They flourish when you become aware of what makes their life possible. You can deploy resources more thoughtfully when you acknowledge that first. In a complex system like a natural garden, the system benefits from the life of its components. This interconnectedness defines the objective: how does the system perpetuate beyond the life support of the gardener?

I'm a big fan of the adaptive management cycle—try out an idea, evaluate how it works, and adjust the practice based on what you learned. This mindset is critical for caring for a natural garden. As resource consumption goes, the human resources of time, patience, and knowledge matter as much in a natural garden as anything plants produce. No amount of effort or money counteracts this. I once overheard a famous designer glibly remark that every client wants a project to be good, fast, and cheap, but only two of those conditions can ever be true at the same time. Always read the terms and conditions.

Complexity

"One could say that biodiversity is shorthand for complexity."
—Emma Marris in *Rambunctious Garden*

The understated freeness of natural, so-called wild places has inspired gardens for centuries. Yet living with a naturally inspired garden becomes an odyssey in increasing complexity. Plants take the lead, a thought that feels like a loss of control and stokes the untamed myth. At this moment, you have to suspend disbelief and dig deeper to understand plants and the life they support.

Natural gardening increases complexity while resolving its outcomes. The journey treads on the road of abundance—you'll always be planting or, at the very least, promoting plants. Adopt the mantra "Just keep planting." Some days, it's an encouraging statement; others, it's a command. If a tree falls, embrace the light and just keep planting. If a plant succumbs to disease, consider why and just keep planting. In our own way and time, planting is one of the most important actions we can take to cultivate greater abundance and complexity in the landscapes we call home.

Natural gardens are not merely do-good contrivances. They can be an essential part of humanity's ecological footprint, an extension of our habitats and ways of living. A natural garden's ample abundance runs counter to the trend: humans tend to homogenize and simplify landscapes as proxies for order and control. How do you become a steward of more? How do you conceive plant-driven habitats for creatures you barely understand?

No matter the design and concept of your current garden, life exists. The garden exists interdependently with its place, a horticultural island in an ecological sea. What at first seems separate would be impossible without its surroundings. Your job is to deepen the mystery. Cultivating a plant-centric perspective requires acknowledging and respecting the lives of plants as more than objects to arrange. They are, in fact, alive, even if largely sedentary. Amplifying their lives, rooted in place, is the key to generating complexity in the landscape. A complex landscape is a habitat and home.

Our Long Look Prairie at Three Oaks Garden (Des Moines, Iowa, US) maximizes plant diversity without compromising the emotional experience. We want to live with a natural garden even when it challenges us to see it.

A Natural Garden Is a Complex System

"The 'chaos' grows on underlying gardening skills."

—Jenks Farmer

Holistic, cyclical, dynamic. Any ecologically attuned gardener tosses around these words fluently—the garden isn't separate from the world around it. Complex systems are greater than the sum of their parts. Understanding the natural garden as a complex system requires knowing more than how individual plant species grow, even if that's where a gardener starts. You have to understand how they interact with their environment.

Emergence is a key signature of complex systems, a big-picture phenomenon where collective patterns and properties arise from the interactions and behaviors of individuals, like the flocking behavior of birds or the social dynamics of anthills. Microclimates, for example, arise from emergent properties of exposure, soil, and the environment. Coexistence is an emergent phenomenon in a stable community of many species, even as individual species flourish, falter, and flow. Emergence resists reduction—you can't simply explain what's happening by looking at one or a few conditions. In nature, individuals are subordinate to the system. A natural garden achieves harmony with its place by elevating plants in unison instead of spotlighting the soloists. The natural garden is full of emergent possibilities.

The nature of the garden is characterized by flexibility and the potential for change. At any moment, a natural garden exhibits an immense number of possible outcomes, both unpredictable and undetermined. Living with a natural garden requires an openness to these possibilities. You can't possibly know or predict every outcome and don't need to.

A natural garden is, first and foremost, self-organizing, an organic well of complexity. At first, a self-organizing garden sounds like a place where vegetation naturally determines its future. To the well-heeled gardener, it sounds like a mess. But the self-organizing garden exists beneath the surface of every planting, a lurking possibility that deals the cards as we roll the dice. This underlying engine produces the raw material for making a natural garden, the plant life that supplants sweat equity. This process is random and determined, shaped by the available resources and how a plant uses them to produce its biomass.

More Is More

Cultivating complexity in your garden challenges the conventional wisdom that "less is more." Good design in modern times places a premium on minimalism and simplicity, a stark contrast to the intricate and multifaceted workings of natural systems. Think baroque, not modernist. Cultivating complexity challenges our traditional beliefs about how plants grow in home landscapes, deviating from a paradigm of order and control to one of chaos and unpredictability; more is more.

As your natural garden grows, the biomass becomes the basis for gardening, the raw material you refine and edit over time. Even when a garden races away with growth, you can always disturb the biomass to bring it back into focus. A sharp blade is handy for managing density, especially if it's not what you've planted or intended.

Managing diversity requires embracing a somewhat unconventional approach, balancing "a lot of a little," "a little of a lot," or just "more of everything." Call it hyperplanting. Critics may wonder when more becomes too much, but the idea of planting with intensity stands as a response to increasingly homogenized landscapes. Complex hotspots of diversity defy blandness, serving as a thread that connects a vaster landscape to your natural garden.

Reducing the abundance of a successful species—like the native North American annual Amphiachyris dracunculoides *(prairie broomweed)—is easier than coaxing a reluctant one.*

As you shape your garden, consider the liminal spaces where plants exceed your control. These areas often become integral to your garden's sense of place and connection to the broader landscape. Some creatures prefer these channels of feral plants, which form an unseen highway that connects one patch to another. If this is a place where plants run amok, consider why. Regeneration simply produces more growth. You have to decide how to value it and what to do.

From the sidewalk crevices to the shady undersides, life moves across this corner of Great Dixter & Gardens in East Sussex.

What Are You Gardening For?

A nature-oriented home garden can make a meaningful difference in preserving local biodiversity because most species live locally. We should do our best to cultivate vibrant habitats for them in real time while being brutally honest about the time frames in which we garden: most horticultural landscapes are ephemeral. While you might strive for endurance, a garden's relative stability is often beyond your control unless you plan to live in the same house and place for decades. Even then, events like utility upgrades, street widenings, home improvement projects, and property fences perturb the otherwise idyllic trajectory of the fantasy natural garden. Don't sweat the disturbances; just keep planting. This attitude reflects what environmental journalist Fred Pearce calls the "abiding traits of real nature—transience, dynamism, and contingency."

In an increasingly disturbed landscape, urban natural gardens can provide resource-rich oases for invertebrates and birds more consistently than in fragmented natural areas. Solid data supports this, although the field is comparatively young and developmental. As a gardener, you likely want to know what to plant. But it's not only *what* you plant but *how* you garden with it. That's the recipe for a vibrant habitat. Conventional wisdom has long championed the exclusive use of native plants in habitat gardens. It's easy to see why—these flora and fauna have evolved in a complex dance over vast stretches of geologic time. We should treasure and conserve those linkages. Planting natives has direct and obvious benefits for biodiversity.

Yet recent insights suggest non-native plants also play a role in these habitats, mainly because many native and non-native plants comprise most urban landscapes today. If we accept the ecological novelty of urban environments today, how do we garden so that more life may flourish? Prioritize planting for usefulness to other creatures.

Native and non-native plants interact in living networks that stretch across cities and countryside. While each group supports different cohorts of organisms, both groups of plants play vital roles in contemporary ecological functions. In comparative trials under controlled circumstances, native plants often attract more individual pollinators and a more comprehensive range of species than non-natives. But in the cultivated, spontaneous, or natural landscapes beyond our homes today, natives and non-natives coexist as a product of human disturbance. While more research is warranted, evidence suggests that non-native garden plants attractive to pollinators already fulfill an ecosystem service when native plant resources are seasonally limited, without adverse effects on plant-pollinator networks. Native animals' ability to utilize non-native species can make these plants integral to their diet in urban settings. Urban faunas tend to be generalists, which may explain why some urban fauna respond neutrally to plant origin.

The ecology of pollination—one of the most significant interactions you can foster and observe in your natural garden—is complicated. There are hundreds of native pollinators, including bees, wasps, flies, butterflies, and moths. Different plant species offer varying nutritional resources for pollinators, and each pollinator species may have general specific preferences for particular plant groups. Generalist pollinators interact with many types of flowers, visiting various plant species to collect nectar and pollen for nutritional gain. Specialist pollinators have

Meadow Nord, our front yard meadow here at Three Oaks Garden (Des Moines, Iowa, US) features over 100 species artfully designed to evoke a prairie clearing in open woods, the sort of plant community that once flourished before our home was built in 1941.

Canopies with multiple layers create more opportunities for nesting and foraging, especially when anchored by keystone natives like Salix nigra *(black willow) at Chanticleer Garden (Wayne, Pennsylvania, US).*

coevolved strong preferences for specific plant groups, often at the level of the plant family. Gardening with a variety of plant species from across different families increases the availability of diverse nutrition sources for a multitude of pollinators.

Bees require flowers for nectar and pollen, and many bee species are generalist consumers of floral resources. Therefore, a mix of native and non-native plants in a garden can increase the number of bee species present. A group of California researchers documented 52 out of 229 bee species collected in their multi-year survey from only non-native plants. All of the 52 bee species were native. Similar results were found in a study in Capitol Reef National Park, Utah, where non-native plant species attracted as many or more native bee species as native plant species. Both studies highlight the roles of native and non-native plants in creating diverse habitats for bees and other pollinators in both urban and rural landscapes. If your goal is to support thriving

bee populations, the research suggests your key criterion when choosing plants should be their attractiveness, regardless of whether native or non-native. The finding alone may not be that surprising, but its applications are limited in the context of a natural garden. In a complex system, you can't simply garden for the benefit of one pollinator species any more than you can tell those pollinators on which plants to feed.

Consider the range of pollinators visiting your garden, even at night when you're perhaps unaware of their existence. Bees and birds garner lots of attention during the day, but new research suggests nighttime visitors like moths may do the lion's share of pollination. Less recognized invertebrate predators like wasps, hoverflies, beetles, and lacewings also require flowers for hunting. Simply because an insect lands on a flower doesn't make it a pollinator. Additionally, the connections between invertebrates, particularly butterflies and their host plants, can take many years to form in garden settings, depending on the species involved and the time it takes to discover your habitat offering. While positive effects can emerge after a decade, you might feel better knowing that timeline upfront.

Animals don't live and interact with the environment predictably. For instance, environments influence their constituents; urban birds and bees behave differently than their rural counterparts. Sometimes, this confounds researchers' attempts to understand them, particularly in places like New York City, where the landscape bears little semblance to its most recent ecological reference. Some studies suggest that an increase in exotic fruit abundance can boost the population of frugivorous birds. However, greater abundances of a few species often come at the expense of species diversity. Non-native plants can also provide structural resources, forming important nesting sites or offering shelter from predators in urban landscapes where little native vegetation remains.

Habitats in heavily developed circumstances filter those organisms that can adapt and utilize the available resources. Put another way, urban environments naturally select the creatures most likely or fit to occur there. Reptiles, for instance, use plants primarily for shelter and show more neutral responses to plant origins, suggesting shelter resources are more related to a plant's growth form. Experimental studies in urban environments have highlighted the importance of non-native flowering plants to bees and butterflies, even when native plants are available. This suggests that the geographic origins of plant species may be less critical for enhancing biodiversity than their functional attributes, including their contribution to the complexity of garden habitats.

You will make your own decisions in your natural garden, informed by experiences with your place and a steadfast curiosity for new insights. Plant more native species, broadly defined by bioregion, but do so with abundance. The underlying message in much of the data from the last decade underscores that more is more. Tucking in a few beloved native species into a corner of the garden may seem virtuous because of their origins, but to make an impact, you must offer more to the creatures in your midst. You can't practice native plant tokenism and expect flourishing results.

New research shows that moths may best bees for the title of most efficient pollinators. Alypia octomaculata *(eight-spotted forester) commonly occur along woodland edges throughout much of eastern North America.*

Similarly, don't reduce the ecosystem value of non-native species to zero simply based on their origins. Whatever your judgment, if already present in the greater mosaic of the existing landscape around your home, these species serve the ecosystem more than nonliving alternatives. Non-native species merit consideration if they complement the phenology of natives and serve the real-time needs of pollinators and other creatures. Think of them as playing a bit part.

Finally, consider the scale of your efforts. At the landscape level, ensuring a continuous offering of floral resources throughout the growing season promotes optimal pollinator abundance. If you already have a large garden with abundant floral resources, you should keep adding flowers at a comparable scale. A tiny dish at the end of a robust buffet doesn't fill many plates, regardless of whether it's better for you. Cultivating a diverse roster of plants in your garden supports local pollinator populations throughout the year at various stages of their lives amid seasonal extremes.

Growing the Garden Habitat

A preoccupation with habitat motivates many natural gardening efforts. Habitats aren't formed from a tidy list of resources—food, water, and shelter—even if their components are reduced to such categories. A habitat is a biological home for any number of species. If gardens are designer ecosystems, why not design something more gracious, inclusive, and forward-looking? Gardens can support high biodiversity despite the negative consequences of urbanization that often precede their creation. Although gardens in urban areas may not be as biodiverse as the native habitats that once occupied the same land, they can still benefit wildlife when managed consciously for their benefit. Every garden, regardless of size, has the potential to be a thriving ecosystem.

If you've spent any time in nature, you've probably stuck your nose in a field guide, searching out the identity of a bird, wildflower, frog, or bug that bedeviled your recall. In many such tomes, the habitat a creature calls home is often reduced to a few spare words—pasture, open fields, fencerows. Imagine an entry for humans. How would you describe human habitat? The question is a bit absurd. Yet, our understanding of organisms operates in these relatively simple terms. While a field guide lists the likely, daresay preferred, habitat that a species most often occurs in, where plants and animals live is less a function of labels and more about how the resources of a place fulfill a creature's needs. How, then, do we create, cultivate, and steward habitats for creatures we know so little about?

Garden Size and Habitat Complexity

The more real estate you have to plant densely and diversely, the better. While small gardens make a difference, maximizing the size of your natural garden will have scalar benefits for the life around you. Spatially extensive, diverse gardens have more resources and niches that support a greater variety of species. Logically, as area increases, more opportunities exist for a greater array of flora and fauna (and what gardener wouldn't take more space for jamming in more plants?). Designed plant communities generally succeed over increasingly larger areas because of their emergent properties; the reproduction of many species in the same area begets the expansion of the whole community.

The boundary of an area also affects which species call that patch home. Ecologists define edge effects as the changes and dynamics that occur at the boundaries of different habitat types. Life thrives on the edge of habitats because it's assorted, ragged, and more spatially complex than the middle. But not all species love the exposure. For some, the distance to the closest edge defines the limits of their home; some prefer to dwell deep in a patch away from all that disturbance. Beetles and woodland birds seem to follow this pattern.

Spatially complex landscapes provide more habitat. In natural communities, plants grow in layers, from the understory to the top of the canopy. Even in resource-limited environments like deserts, you can still find layered oases of plants that congregate around pools of water and nutrients. Each layer, regardless of scale, animates the environment, creating opportunities for different organisms to feed, shelter, and reproduce. When studied at the ecosystem scale, the extent of vegetation cover correlates positively with the abundance and diversity of arthropods and vertebrates. This suggests that simply increasing the amount of vegetation in your garden impacts biodiversity positively (especially so if that vegetation is useful to a great many species). Unsurprisingly, the recipe better predicts the meal than the ingredient list alone. But ignoring a species' origin can limit the effectiveness of this approach. Human-dominated landscapes tend to feature mostly generalist animals that thrive amid greater disturbance and resource availability. Increasingly, though, urban areas are

Strategus antaeus (ox beetle) *feeds on leaves and fruits as adults, burrowing deep into the sandy ground with trowel-like legs to nest.*

becoming the last outposts for rarer species pushed from rural areas due to agriculture and development. Therefore, it's crucial to consider resource-specific relationships when planning our gardens, even when most fauna rely on a relative handful of abundant plant species. But how do you know who's coming for dinner and what they want to eat?

What Gets In?

Biodiversity gets a lot of street cred in the world today. But how much biodiversity *should* exist on a parcel of land stands starkly perpendicular to the science of what *can* or even *does*. A lack of biodiversity spells trouble, according to a mountain of compelling evidence worldwide. As a gardener, how many plant species should you grow to support an abundant array of creatures?

To a large extent, the context of where you garden already defines the fauna your natural garden supports. Ecologists call this environmental filtering, the process by which only certain species can survive and thrive in a particular environment while others cannot. Environmental filters like temperature, rainfall, soil type, and availability of resources select for organisms that can adapt. In other words, the features of the landscape where you live—urban, suburban, or rural—define the nature of your place today.

In recent years, attention-grabbing headlines about endangered bees finding refuge in small urban gardens propagate the message that even small plots harbor outsized ecological benefits. But these creatures didn't just fly in on a vacation package. They were already there, perhaps lurking in the shadows or a nearby plot. Their limited abundance underscores an ecological reality—most species are uncommon.

Measures of biodiversity aren't equal from garden to garden, even in the same region. What one gardener might consider a reasonable number of plant species to grow, another might consider a starting point. Thus, judgments about the breadth of species growing in a garden deserve context. Is your garden surrounded by open, natural space or hemmed in by urban development? Is it a well-stitched patch or an oasis? Upon realizing that your natural garden adds to the complexity of the landscape, you can begin to consider its contribution to your surroundings. Compared to the common alternative—monocultural swathes of lawns—the results are apparent in many studies: small gardens planted abundantly with dense vegetation support more insects. When comparing habitat patches to one another, though, the results can be strikingly different.

Pycnanthemum muticum *(smooth mountain mint)* supports a dizzying blur of insects, including butterflies, bees, flies, and wasps, all of whom use some part of the plant's floral display to complete their lives.

Gardening for Life

Planting makes habitat; gardening keeps it alive. As described in this book, natural gardens thrive with the disturbance of seasonally infrequent activities, which can counter cycles of drought, extreme weather, and other natural phenomena. With the system in mind, the keystone gardener can steer the landscape through short-term events fostering its fauna. Regardless of the complexity of the habitat you grow today, you can make considerable changes to the status quo by adopting a lighter touch. Horticultural disturbances like frequent lawn mowing, fertilizer, and pesticide application reduce biodiversity and amount to needless fussing in a natural garden beyond reasonable allowances for kicking a ball or bouncing on a trampoline.

As you proceed with your natural gardening, be aware of the intensity and duration of disturbances in your vicinity, such as land conversions for agriculture and commercial activities. In regions with longer histories of agriculture and more variable natural environments, specific bird communities have adapted and become more resilient to land-use changes. Species that can tolerate deforestation tend to be smaller, migratory, less dependent on mature natural forests, and more flexible regarding food resources. The abundance of these organisms today reflects their successful adaptations to the modern world. On the other hand, areas with shorter agricultural histories and more stable environmental conditions, such as remote regions of North America or tropical zones in the global south, are hotspots for significant land use changes. Preserving intact landscapes in these regions is crucial to maintaining complete species assemblages and preventing further loss of sensitive species. Conservation is always more effective when preserving existing biodiversity first instead of attempting to restore it later.

Gardens play a critical role in amplifying the abundance of nature in their midst, supporting the migration and reproduction of species quietly going about their business. If gardens are only refuges, it implies that anything beyond them is inhospitable. In reality, gardens increase nature's housing stock. Whether creating a new natural garden or restoring an existing one, your efforts benefit the local communities, which can reap even greater rewards from enhanced connections.

Planting makes habitat; gardening keeps it alive. Melissodes communis *(common long-horned bee) foraging pollen on a flower of* Iliamna remota *(Kankakee mallow).*

Think of a hedgerow like a child's earnest artwork—a fascinating scribble that reveals more than it first suggests. The hedgerow connects your garden to a wilder beyond, even if it's hard to visualize.

Connection

Habitat connectivity should factor into the design and stewardship of your natural garden. Connecting habitats allows for the movement of wildlife, facilitating essential processes like foraging, breeding, and genetic exchange. Gardens are well-documented dispersal corridors for small mammals, insects, and birds. Amphibians and reptiles probably benefit, although these groups tend to be underrepresented in ecological studies in urban environments. These connections enable organisms to access resources, adapt to changing conditions, and maintain healthy populations.

There's an old saying that good fences make good neighbors. While necessary and practical for many reasons, many fences and hard, manufactured boundaries block the movements of flightless natural neighbors. Most species benefit from organic, irregular boundaries between habitats. A living network probably already exists on your street, whether you can detect the linkages. These green bridges allow local fauna to move and thrive, whether at ground level or high up in the canopy. Through planting and stewardship, your goal is to enhance the connection—plant the road with resources that organisms can utilize in their daily lives.

Admittedly, porosity isn't always practical at all stages of a natural garden's development. Even as you restrict the movement of some herbivorous mammals (like deer) early in the life of a new planting, you'll want to consider how these creatures move through your garden over the long haul. Areas with intense deer pressure reflect human disturbances to the landscape and may fluctuate independently of your efforts to plant a species-rich habitat. The best means for living with intense herbivory may be to keep it out, but this is rarely a resilient or inexpensive solution. In the big picture, a porous boundary is a good goal whenever possible, so long as the plantings have established the capacity to regenerate after something takes a hit.

Habitat Gardening

Garden ecology is complex. As you steward your natural garden, keep an open mind to new findings and methods. Much of what we know about the ecological role of gardens comes from research done in the Global North and with a strong bias for birds and insects. We know comparatively little about how reptiles and amphibians use gardens, even as many gardeners know of them in their midst. Perhaps most humbling is that few studies have looked empirically at the value of ecological gardening methods relative to purported results. Inferentially, many of these practices derive from larger-scale restoration work, but as illustrated here, patch size introduces variation in how organisms live and interact with their surroundings.

Conversely, encouraging more gardeners to engage with natural gardening techniques gives the world more examples to study—diversify and densify your plantings with native and functionally valuable species, swear off pesticides, and harness disturbance as a tool, not a routine. Each of your natural gardens contributes to the richness of its mosaic, especially when connected physically, branch to branch and path to trail. The question is precisely how and for how long. As gardens come and go, those that age with the patina of place become more integrated into the fabric of the landscape, evolving in the frame of a bigger picture than your backyard.

Lichens and mosses form verdant patinas on hard and organic surfaces in natural gardens.

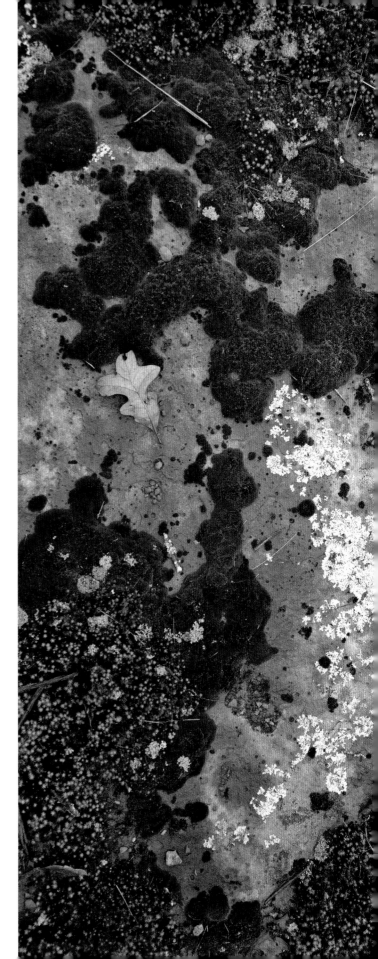

Creature Features

Within your neighborhood or region, factors like the amount of urbanized versus open space, number of trees, and extent of natural vegetation dramatically filter the types of biodiversity you'll find in your garden. While you may not be able to restructure the whole macro landscape, you can enhance the complexity and composition of your garden. The physical features of your landscape in total, including its soil, predict the composition and complexity of animal communities that call your garden home.

The following list of garden-scale habitat features derives from global landscape ecology studies with notes about the creatures supported. These features support faunal life and essential ecosystem services like pollination, herbivory, seed dispersal, and soil development. Evaluate and consider how you could add or enhance these features through continued site-specific interventions. Of note, the primary habitat feature not listed here is the availability of water, which generally benefits most carbon-based life forms.

Bare Ground: Areas in the garden where the soil or ground lacks vegetation or plant cover.

- Ground-nesting bees and beetles require exposed soil to make nests.
- Many ground-nesting bird species also require open or sparsely vegetated areas for foraging and raising broods.
- Some amphibians breed in open areas near water sources.

Grass Cover: The extent or proportion of the garden area covered by grasses, including turfgrasses and open grassland vegetation.

- Lawn areas can be detrimental for some bird species, while others require open areas for foraging.
- Herbivore abundance increases with grass cover, presumably because these species forage on vegetation that is amenable to grazing and occurs at higher abundances in open or edge areas.

- Extensive lawn area is negatively associated with overall biodiversity, often in connection with management practices.

Rock Cover: The garden area covered by rocks, stones, or hardscape surfaces.

- Many invertebrates like beetles, ground-nesting wasps, and bees require unobstructed stone or hard surfaces and crevices to build nests and raise larvae.
- Reptiles and amphibians shelter under rocks or hard surfaces during hot or dry conditions.
- Lichens and mosses pioneer ecosystems, colonizing rocks, concrete, and hard surfaces, trapping moisture and organic material that provides habitat for tiny arthropods.

Decaying Biomass: Organic matter in various stages of decomposition.

- Decomposers are abundant in high amounts of compost, grass clippings, recycled wood, and leaf litter. Their abundance increases with increasing land area, larger trees, and shaded understories.
- For predatory wasps, environments with complex leaf litter, thatch, and mulch foster their abundance.
- Spider abundance has been shown to increase with mulch cover.

Forb Cover and Richness: The diversity and extent of forb species present within the garden habitat.

- Generalist, abundant plant species support general and specialist pollinators more consistently than rare plants.
- Foraging activity for honeybees and bumblebees increases with the abundance of a single forb species (i.e., a single large flower area produced by a single species). However, this effect diminishes with more excellent landscape disturbance (such as in urban or developed areas).
- Most research shows positive relationships between overall floral abundance and bee abundance, although local trends may reveal nuances. Honeybee abundance is generally higher in sites with larger floral patches,

whereas overall bee species richness and diversity increased with more clustered floral resources. Notably, some studies show that the arrangement of floral resources and the connectivity between patches is as important as the number of individuals or species of flowering plants.

- Spiders are found less often in garden areas with high forb richness, seeming to prefer areas with fewer flowering plant species.

Tree Number and Size: The count of individual trees and size classes within the garden environment, including height, canopy spread, and trunk diameter.

- Larger trees provide nesting sites and shelter for species like owls, hawks, and eagles, while smaller trees and shrubs offer habitat for songbirds, such as sparrows, warblers, and finches.

- Caterpillars of butterflies and moths often rely heavily on specific tree species as host plants. Notably, *Quercus* (oaks) rank high worldwide for supporting biodiversity.

- Spatially complex tree stands provide countless microhabitats for various insects, from ground-nesting bees to larger bumblebees, honeybees, and predatory insects.

- Tree-dwelling mammals use trees for nesting or foraging.

Woody Species Richness and Structure: The diversity and composition of woody plant species in garden-scale plant communities.

- The spatial structure of vegetation within urban gardens can influence bird species diversity, with high variability supporting greater diversity.

- Plant composition in urban gardens significantly affects bird communities, with high coverage of shrubs and trees important for native and migrating birds.

Total Vegetation Cover: The overall coverage of all plant types, including grasses, forbs, shrubs, and trees, across the garden space.

- Plant cover is a net positive for most organisms.

- Ant species richness is lower in gardens than in natural areas, but ants that adapt to garden environments thrive abundantly.

- Beetle species richness is higher in gardens. Researchers have hypothesized that this may be due to disturbances in garden environments that keep beetle communities diverse and complex compared to natural areas.

- Natural predators, like spiders and many vertebrates, prefer complex vegetated areas and decline as land becomes bare.

Umbrella Policy

There is a timelessness to the environmentalism of planting trees. The health and status of tree canopies consume neighborhood association agendas and propagate small talk among the arboriculturally conscious. For many, trees *are* the nearest and most relatable proxy to nature. They frame views from windows at work and home, offer shade in parking lots, and provide a cool canopy for strolling along sidewalks. Thus, tree planting, not unlike planting in general, is a uniquely human expression of well-being for nature at large. Nobody plants intending to harm.

Planting a future tree canopy serves selfish purposes. Trees provide humanity with a litany of ecosystem services—clean, cooler air chief among them—the sort we need more of in a warming world. In many cities, urban forestry is now seen as essential infrastructure that requires regular and routine investment and that homeowners are encouraged to participate in. More rigorous treatments exist elsewhere, delving into the arguments about where trees belong, who and what they benefit, and why climate policy shouldn't rest solely on the limbs and boughs of urban forests.

At a residential scale, investing in a diverse canopy serves as a literal and environmental umbrella policy for life closer to the ground with cascading benefits. Tree canopies buffer air temperature and humidity extremes closer to the ground, a net positive for humans living in those understories. Trees and their understory associates also lower soil temperature, increasing the soil's capacity to store carbon, a mechanism that becomes even more effective with age and under extreme climate conditions. Green, living infrastructure delivers.

Calls for a more diverse street tree canopy have only increased as introduced pests and diseases ravage former monocultures. Diverse tree populations can enhance local biodiversity beyond that offered in fragmented, natural stands. Planting diversely doesn't seem like complicated advice, particularly for species with abbreviated lifespans. Popular landscape trees like those in the genera *Alnus* (alder), *Betula* (birch), *Salix* (willow), and *Populus* (poplar) often adapt readily to urban environmental conditions but with the tradeoff of living fast and dying young. Long-lived tree genera like *Quercus* (oaks), *Carya* (hickory), *Pinus* (pine), and *Picea* (spruce) often require a greater investment in their establishment, if nothing more than time and patience. Planting diverse tree stands doesn't need to be a collector's exercise but rather a rational attempt at establishing plants that contribute to local ecology over their (hopefully) long lives.

You should think about plant diversity as more than just different species' identities. The features that make them unique or similar, like the diversity of growth habits and life histories, matters too. Consider the many understory trees planted for their seasonal floral displays or size. These trees often experience lower mortality rates at the population level than overstory species, presumably due to reduced solar radiation and lower water requirements. Their niche gives them an advantage. Research on drought resiliency in forests has shown that tree stands with diverse life histories experience less mortality and loss of biomass during extreme droughts. When trees hold onto biomass, they keep carbon locked up longer.

A historic Platanus occidentalis *(American sycamore) with towering proportions at Stoneleigh Garden (Villanova, Pennsylvania, US).*

Just Keep Planting

Think of gardening as a form of ongoing design. Whatever idea you start with will surely evolve as you embrace complexity. While you may borrow inspiration from naturally occurring plant communities and habitats, dispense quickly with any ideas of perfection or purity. Think of your creativity as part of the randomness of nature, even if you use many of the same plants.

Gardening with plant communities provides an opportunity for ongoing planting. The concept of plant communities arose in early twentieth-century plant ecology, developing from an awareness that plants do not grow individually but rather form assemblages with other plant species based on environmental conditions and interactions. A plant community is a diverse assortment of species coexisting in time and place while responding dynamically to their environment. Researchers categorize plant communities in a multitude of ways, ranging from their "social" structure to those associated with otherwise rare species and habitats. Labels and categories abound. They are inherently emergent and in flux, giving rise to unfolding complexity, a beautiful feedback loop you can participate in—just keep planting.

The state of a plant community at any given moment isn't deterministic but rather the result of a complex array of circumstances, some of which, as gardeners, we can influence through design and stewardship. While plant communities are a useful construct for designing and gardening naturalistically, their development in the landscape is the result of time, process, and method.

Like any mantra, there are some exceptions. Planting is disturbance and constantly rooting around in the garden like a feral scavenger restlessly in search of a design vision isn't exactly the goal. I recall a gardening mentor from my childhood who would proudly declare that if she was unsatisfied with a plant, she'd move it. I always wondered what she did about the hole she left behind.

*A trio of ruderal, short-lived species—*Verbascum, Glaucium, *and* Phacelia—*stitch up the disturbed edges of planting areas along paths. Planting design by Mike Kintgen, Denver Botanic Garden.*

This desert plant community, defined by the stress-tolerant shrub Larrea tridentata *(creosote bush)*, springs to life when cool temperatures coincide with abundant rainfall. Ruderal forbs like Salvia columbariae *(chia sage)* and Eschscholzia minutiflora *(pygmy poppy)* form populations of thousands of individuals.

Plants Are Connected to Place

Plant communities illustrate the interconnectedness of plant species with the phenomenon of place. The plant communities that develop in our gardens emerge from what we've planted, hopefully growing into something that looks intentional. But even well-considered designs produce early surprises in the first few growing seasons. If a handful of species depart the system, the voids leave a vacuum for other plant species to exploit. If your planting is diverse enough, you may find other designed species filling in. You may also find unwelcome intruders seizing the opportunity.

All of these aboveground interactions have underground antecedents. In recently disturbed settings, such as those in the aftermath of new home construction, soils can take decades to recover microorganism diversity and abundance. While this disturbance hardly renders them inert, it does shape and predict the kinds of plant communities that develop on those soils in the years after planting. Research published in *Nature Communications* (2023) found evidence for unique fungal interactions between different species in a complex natural community. Absent disturbance, each species cultivated its own microbial entourage, which led to a more stable and orderly community. In disturbed settings, these networks were jumbled together, probably because one or a few species colonized the environment quickly. In garden soils, where disturbance is generally high due to tillage or amendment, it could take years for these dynamic communities of microorganisms to reassemble.

Gardening with plant communities is inherently less species-specific. In a plant community, the whole is greater than the sum of the parts, and understanding how this system of plants grows and changes requires understanding its components as well as the interactions between them. The timing of your activities becomes more seasonal rather than prescribed by the lifecycle of a single species. In gardening with plant communities, you may find that individual species still warrant actions in a unique time frame, but these are exceptions to the rule. Take, for instance, many species of the aster family that benefit from a mid-season cutback. Horticulturally, this improves their shape and prevents them from growing into an unruly mess. But ecologically, the result reduces the biomass of those plants so that they do not outcompete other species in the community. While this activity might seem tailored to these species, the community benefits.

The Referee

In cooperation with your growing environment, you become a referee of the ecological garden. While it's easy to blame or praise plants for their behavior, most plants don't move much. If a plant doesn't perform as you expect, consider what properties of the environment might contribute to these behaviors. If it's too aggressive, what resources did it take advantage of? If it died, what resources did it lack to succeed? In the former, soil fertility is often a lurking culprit, resulting from well-intended fussing that someone once thought valuable for supporting plant life. While plants require nutrients to grow, too often, traditional gardening activities like fertilizing and sometimes even composting have created richly artificial environments. While fertility is valuable for raising crops and producing yields, it often works against the goals of ecological gardening by reducing overall diversity in favor of those plants that can co-opt nutrients the fastest. What aggressive plant species lack in maliciousness, they make up for with savvy physiology that predisposes them to success over their neighbors.

Patchwork plant communities like this example from the Rock and Alpine Garden, Denver Botanic Gardens (Denver, Colorado, US) thrive in low-resource environments that minimize overcompetition and promote ample diversity.

When gardening with plant communities, your first goal is to preserve diversity. Keep as many species in the game as possible. Planting diversely offers a form of ecological insurance, which tends to accumulate in value over the life of the landscape. Diverse plant communities regulate their environment and experience less drastic fluctuations in temperature and relative humidity. These synergies facilitate survival and moderate the effects of mortality across the community. The success of any one species is primarily due to its fitness to the place, including relationships with its neighbors. For instance, consider understory trees that naturally grow with overhead competition. Used as a specimen without a canopy, an individual plant is exposed to competition, predation, or other environmental pressure. Isolation comes at a cost.

If one or a few threaten to homogenize the plant community, focus on managing those species first. If you garden to promote life, don't extend the leash to species that prohibit others from flourishing. Consider removing their seed heads or limiting how far they spread in a single growing season. You could remove them from the planting altogether and allow other less competitive species to take their place. While monocultural stands of some plant species have ecological benefits (consider wetlands with massive stands of tall grasses, reeds, and other highly competitive plants that hold soil in place), this rarely aligns with the goals of a residential landscape. In a smaller garden, a mosaic patchwork of plant diversity becomes more manageable and desirable than large colonial stands of aggressive species.

The Promoter

Most garden plant communities assemble over time as new plants join the community than from defined niches as seen in nature. Communities form based on the species that thrived initially, with natural forces adjusting their abundance and compressing their niches to match the resources available. Beyond refereeing, your second goal is to promote abundance. Apart from fostering new plantings (more on that in the next essay), support the plants you already have by allowing them to thrive; growth is a good thing. While most garden plantings won't persist in their designed form (or even at all) for decades, it's worth remembering that many plants are capable of living and thriving on longer time frames than we perceive in gardens. A garden offers only a fleeting glimpse of plants in the moment.

Species with ruderal tendencies, like reseeding annuals and biennials, fluctuate wildly in abundance from year to year. This phenomenon has many causes, with species variously responding to drought or limited resources, a lack of competition from other species, or simply succeeding due to chance alone. Some species take several years to emerge and mature from the last seed set, extending generation time between reproductively mature individuals. Reseeding isn't so bad—you should be glad something is perpetuating and aspire to understand why.

Conversely, some plants bide their time, taking years to establish in a planting while life happens around them. Woody plants fit this profile as do deeply rooted perennials with significant underground biomass. If planted in low abundance, they often assume a more structural or feature role in plantings. If you desire more for a particular effect, never mind what you didn't know at planting, and add a few more later.

Celebrate different outcomes even if you use the same methods; a lack of sameness isn't *better* or *worse*. As you observe a planting in the years following establishment, monitor the edges for the greatest rates of mortality. Edges are always more prone to disturbance relative to the core of a shape, a rule that applies to individual species groupings and the landscape as a whole. The Irish garden designer and author Helen Dillon wrote, "If you keep the edges tidy, nobody minds the messy middle."

Intermingling plant communities form the living weft of the natural garden throughout the seasons. Two asters—Symphyotrichum oblongifolium 'Dream of Beauty' (Dream of Beauty aromatic aster) and S. ericoides (frost aster)—flicker into autumn through the fading leaves of Ruellia humilis (prairie petunia).

Focus on the Seasons

While diversity and abundance keep plant communities functional, how do those elements fill out the garden's calendar? How does the designed plant community weather the seasons year in and year out? As you observe plant growth, document when they emerge and when they flower. You'll be amazed at how much these events change from year to year. Knowing when plants bloom serves both horticultural and ecological purposes, particularly in climates with distinct seasons. You can keep each month in aesthetic focus while also knowing when resources peak and wane for the creatures who depend on them.

I never understood why some gardeners were totally obsessed with how long something bloomed. In college, I worked for a time as a copywriter for a horticultural printing company, wordsmithing cultural information and plant descriptions into the tiny margins of a plastic hang tag. I hammered out the same rote phrases to describe duration—long-blooming, ever-blooming, blooms all season, etc. Why not embrace the spectacle of a brief affair? Nature offers them readily. In a diverse planting scheme, one or a few species may carry the seasonal banner, but the parade of diversity continues. So long as there is a unifying theme in each season, maximal diversity is possible.

As you keep up with the calendar, consider the journey of each plant through the season, from when it breaks dormancy to its maximal flowering and, finally, its senescence. In northern temperate climates, autumn is a great time of year for scrutinizing biomass. After living with it through a growing year, you can assess the sum of any visual conflicts. Whereas in southerly places, fall is a new spring on the heels of an insufferable summer. The arrival of the cool season kick-starts a new year of life and planting. Flip the script as geographically appropriate.

The horticulture team at the Lurie Garden (Chicago, Illinois, US) keeps a running tally of when and how long plants bloom. Annually, they compile a list of plants that bloomed for 100 days or more, which they playfully dub "The 100 Club." Long-blooming North American natives like *Callirhoe involucrata* (purple poppy mallow) and *Sanguisorba canadensis* (Canadian burnet) have made the list in recent years. In the case of the Lurie Garden, many of these species grow in populations; far from a clump or two, these species repeat abundantly throughout the Piet Oudolf–designed planting scheme or grow in large colonies. Sometimes scale helps. But the task of keeping track is something any gardener can do, no matter the size of the landscape. The data from year to year acts as your own microcosm on the flowering patterns of plants in your region.

Save room for intimate, ephemeral moments in the garden. Plants like this Dodecatheon meadia *(shooting stars) deserve close inspection.*

Penstemon *'Midnight Masquerade' (Midnight Masquerade beardtongue) serves as a valuable player through three seasons in this planting, shifting roles as others come into focus like in this midsummer vignette with* Agastache foeniculum *(anise hyssop) and* Pycnanthemum tenuifolium *(slender mountain mint).*

Extending the season in a natural garden gives every feature of the plant aesthetic value. These vignettes from the Lurie Garden (Chicago, Illinois, US) showcase designer Piet Oudolf's masterful treatment of vogue senescence.

Why is organic matter on the ground called "litter" when plants put it there instead of humans? If we put it there, suddenly it's "mulch." In a natural garden, nobody should mind when plants don't pick up after themselves.

Make Plants Grow

Beyond soil, water, and light, have you ever wondered what makes plants grow? Ecologists define amplitude as the range of conditions plants can adapt to while carrying on vital functions. Some species have narrow requirements—like the North American cliff-dwelling *Asplenium rhizophyllum* (walking fern)—that limit how readily they can grow in anything beyond their native habitats. Ecologists call these *specialists*. Conversely, *generalists* grow almost anywhere, broadly adaptable to the environment's whims.

Plant growth is constrained by anything that limits productivity, such as low fertility or the lack of water. From an agronomic point of view, amplifying resource access is a good thing. As a gardener striving to promote a diverse array of plants in a physically abbreviated environment, you want to use stress to your advantage. Too much of a good thing could quickly produce more growth than you can wrangle. While beneficial for ecology, a good gardener might wince.

You have to establish a plant for it to persist. A garden habitat won't magically appear if the plants you recruit for the task don't survive beyond the first season. This establishment period features its own rules, even if you still adopt a low-input mentality. Resource consciousness is admirable but best measured against well-established plantings, not those struggling to persist. Establishment may take longer in extreme stress, like an extended drought. I call these "mass years," a growing season set aside for biomass generation, where expectations are reasonable, and disturbance is minimal, generally invoked in the early years of establishment or following a more intensive window of disturbance.

Mulch

Mulching offers obvious benefits, such as moisture retention, weed suppression, and soil protection. However, there are trade-offs associated with frequent mulching, a strangely routine habit in traditional gardens. One significant issue is the carbon-to-nitrogen (C:N) ratio imbalance. Organic mulches, like wood chips or bark, are high in carbon, which initially ties up nitrogen as it decomposes. This can temporarily deprive plants of nitrogen, affecting their growth. Few plants have evolved in the company of shredded wood.

Plantings of almost every stripe and location make their own mulch after an initial season, provided the organic matter accumulates for the benefit of the soil. Traditional gardening often judiciously interrupts this process. When considering mulch in an ecological context, the critical question is its purpose and duration. Mulch is particularly advantageous for new plantings, aiding weed suppression and moisture conservation. However, as a planting matures, the need for mulch diminishes, as the accumulated biomass serves as natural mulch over time, if necessary or desirable. When desirable, embrace the mulch plants freely offer and skip whatever comes in a bag.

Different types of mulch, such as shredded hardwoods or mineral mulch, cater to different

In resource-rich environments, lush ground planes act as living mulch for a designed plant community.

environments, with the goal being rapid decomposition and infrequent use or application. In meadow and woodland environments, excess biomass may require removal to prevent smothering and suppressing desirable plants. If you mulch during the establishment period, opt for materials with lower carbon-to-nitrogen ratios, such as compost, shredded leaves, or organic matter en route to decomposition. Apply it thinly. If the planting features an ample matrix layer—think green mulch—you won't need to mulch for more than the first season of growth.

Bicolors, selfs, and shades in between. This garden population of Ratibida columnifera *(upright coneflower) displays the range of natural variation found within wild populations.*

Protecting New Plantings from Herbivory

Herbivory happens. You can curse the deer and shoo off the rabbits, but the creatures who graze the landscape for sustenance will eventually return to the buffet you've planted. As you garden with the nature of place, the long-term goal is not to create some pristine environment that controls only a subset of wildlife but rather to create a landscape that fosters the diversity of life. In urban environments, some herbivores relish our company, perhaps even too much for their own good. Left unchecked, this dance between food and the population it supports operates like supply and demand. Eventually, due to overconsumption, the supply runs low, and animal populations crash or move along. Nature operates cyclically.

Protecting your new plantings often requires only a temporary intervention. The goal is to establish plantings until they have enough reserves to recover from browsing. While most herbivory is rarely fatal, it can disfigure woody species with determinate growth habits. You'll want to protect these trees and shrubs for a few seasons until their branches become undesirably mature for most browsers. Nothing is foolproof, so gamble with time and odds accordingly.

If you have a large area you've just planted and a considerable supply of lumber, you might get creative and build a slash wall. Imagine a fortress built from repurposed logs that protect vulnerable young transplants from the relentless nibbling of deer. Instead of letting leftover logs and branches—known as slash—go to waste after a forest harvest, they become life-saving barriers up to 10 feet (3 m) tall and wide. The introduction of slash walls effectively deters deer, providing a haven for plants to flourish and establish. In research done at Cornell University, slash walls have allowed protected seedlings to grow as much as 30 percent more in a single season when compared to unprotected seedlings. Moreover, the slash walls offer habitat benefits for various wildlife species—think of them as extensive hedgerows—and cost approximately one-third that of traditional fencing. Excluding herbivory for as long as possible maximizes successful planting establishment at a high level of diversity.

Natural Selection

Natural selection operates continuously in gardens, often giving rise to new plant varieties through chance seedlings. However, the dynamics of natural selection in gardens differ from those in natural habitats. Various selection pressures and environmental gradients unique to gardens influence how plants grow and reproduce. Additionally, differences in pollinator communities between wild habitats and gardens can impact the effectiveness of pollination services. Observing and understanding natural selection in gardens is a valuable tool for ecological gardeners.

When managing seedlings that appear in your garden, there is no universal standard for genetic diversity within populations. The level of genetic diversity varies between species and even populations of the same species. For instance, dandelions and similar species may have minimal genetic diversity within populations, with all dandelions in a yard potentially being clones due to a phenomenon known as apomixis (asexual seed formation). While this might seem exceptional, it highlights how nature adapts to different environments and stresses. Sometimes, a single clone can have the highest genetic fitness in a particular environment, indicating that evolution is fundamentally adaptive and context-dependent. In ecological terms, a garden is subject to scale effects, where the probability of ecosystem change due to chance alone is influenced by its size. Asexually propagated cultivars that thrive in gardens do so against the odds. Their success is a testament to the complex interplay between genetics, environmental factors, and adaptation within the unique microcosm of a garden.

Seeding Around

Some years back, I looked across a garden population of *Echinacea paradoxa*, the paradoxically yellow cone-flower in a genus of pink and white, and noticed some flowers displayed curious tints of lemon and cream while others approached shades of gold and orange. This natural nuance, chance hybrids arising from bees moving between multiple species and varieties in my garden, didn't shake the planet or make me any money. But noticing it underscores one way humans have interacted with plants throughout our existence. Whether corn for consumption or roses for regalia, plants valued by humans exist in tension between nature and culture. How can we recognize the value of plants based on their contribution to an ecosystem, rather than just their appearance or edibility?

Scholar Noel Kingsbury explored these issues in his deft account of the history of human plant breeding, *Hybrid* (2011). He writes: "At first glance, life in the wild . . . and life in cultivation . . . may seem very different. However, at root, they are the same, as both are subject to evolutionary pressures. On the one hand it is nature that provides this pressure, on the other it is us, the human race."

Taking note of variation and celebrating it comes naturally to gardeners with keen eyes. You should garden to promote it. Permit species with a natural penchant for reseeding the opportunity to do so. Genetic variation within and between populations of organisms gives life its very grist, especially with increasing degrees of environmental change. Through the ecological lens, it's merely an ingredient in the recipe for ecosystem function. As in the kitchen, the quality of the ingredients matter. All variation isn't equal, which is a good argument for having as much of it as possible. You can't know what traits might be necessary for plant adaptation in a changing world. You can grow plants from seed, several cultivars of the same species, or in the same genus and achieve a kaleidoscope of variation even in a small garden. Over time, depending on the reproductive biology of the species in question, a population of descendants with rich ancestry may develop, a landrace or a seed strain, by alternate names.

Nowadays, coneflowers have a notorious and categorical reputation for forming hybrids. Commercial hybrids in the early 2000s were inspired by wild-occurring examples of the same, long documented when species like *Echinacea paradoxa* (yellow coneflower), *E. purpurea* (purple coneflower), and *E. simulate* (Ozarks coneflower) crossed paths. While the horticulture industry became enthralled with novelty, stretching from double flowers to retina-searing colors, the humble wild forbearers colorfully illustrate that variation can exist beyond the scope of our understanding. Perhaps these hybrids offer these lineages a way forward into the future. Maybe it's nothing more than genetic white noise.

Perhaps most importantly, you should know what these plants do in your garden. Consider:

- Do they flower abundantly and for an extended period?

- Do you observe pollinators visiting them in bloom?

- Do you observe holes in their leaves or other evidence of herbivory?

These are reasonable questions you can answer with casual observation. Even those wild and crazy coneflowers you spent too much money on will produce viable seedlings that will eventually drift towards resembling their ancestors after many years. As plant species prone to outcrossing, they can't do this independently; instead, they require interactions with pollinating insects.

In the end, reproduction is key to resiliency. If plants aren't reproducing or regenerating, their long-term performance is limited by how long a single individual in a population lives. To put it another way, if plants aren't reproducing, what more do you have than a dusty museum collection?

Naturally occurring Echinacea *hybrids inspired feverish horticultural plant breeding.*

Seed is cost-effective and scalable to projects of various sizes. Compared to planting, it's the least disruptive but also more unpredictable.

Plugs, like those shown here, give many species the right balance of roots to shoots for fast and efficient establishment.

The Mechanics of Planting

As you design and steward a natural garden, the future unfolds in three ways. There's the garden you designed, the one that was established, and the one that persists after many years. In almost every circumstance, each version is different. Ideally, your goal is to minimize the variance or at least not compromise the integrity of your designed planting.

Different strategies exist for establishing plant communities, with advantages and trade-offs for each. Plantings offer greater aesthetic control and faster establishment compared to seedings. On the other hand, seedings are less resource-intensive and more cost-effective for larger-scale projects. Practically speaking, no matter which option you take, the goal is to catalyze the planting's emergent properties. Do you get more out than what you put in?

Consider the trade-offs for how to promote plant growth. Plants that establish first have a home-field advantage. This phenomenon applies to intentionally planted species and existing vegetation, including potential weed species. By examining the existing vegetation on a site, you can infer the challenges that new plantings may face

Larger pots offer immediate gratification and give new transplants a size advantage over existing, robust vegetation.

When planting from a pot larger than a plug, take a few extra seconds to remove as much loose potting media as possible. Soilless, peat-based potting media can prohibit microbial colonization and slow the establishment of new roots.

and decide how best to promote your desirable plant palette. If existing vegetation is robust and productive, you will want to ensure your new plants are fairly matched against the competition. Larger pots offer instant biomass that could improve the odds. If your site is barren, you can adopt a smaller input like plugs or seeds. Smaller plug-sized plants often have a better root-to-shoot ratio and exhibit faster establishment rates than larger specimens. Despite their smaller size, plug-sized plants can accumulate biomass quickly, catching up to larger plants within a single growing season and making them cost-effective by comparison.

Timing also plays a crucial role in the establishment process. For plantings, match the effort to the weather and the calendar; plant when resources are plentiful and environmental conditions are optimal. Planting during the cooler months when soil moisture levels are higher reduces water stress on newly planted seedlings. For seedings, time sowings accordingly. Some species have specific requirements for germination, such as cold stratification or exposure to fluctuating temperatures. Seeds that require cold stratification should be sown in late autumn or early winter to take advantage of natural temperature fluctuations versus seeds that can germinate under ambient conditions.

Pesticides and Fertilizers

Gardeners live with the impact of chemicals whether they've applied any or not. The modern world grew from an extracted and synthesized foundation of chemicals that have amplified agricultural production by controlling plant life. Herbicides neutralize the species that threaten us; fertilizers boost the species that benefit us. The legacy of the Green Revolution, which dramatically transformed agricultural production to feed a rapidly growing global population, includes discomforting realities of soil and water degradation, loss of biodiversity, and a contribution to the homogenization of the landscape. The same movement that allowed for human flourishing enabled ecological deterioration.

You could think of resistance in weeds and insects as nature's rebuttal to human chemistry. Bad actors, in agronomic terms, now run on a pesticide treadmill, jousting with chemists to engineer more combative products. This quest to subdue untamable life ends in finite ecological terms, even as the game seems impossible to quit. An objective, well-meaning bench scientist would say plants showed them how to do it all in the first place. Allelopathic species like black walnuts (*Juglans nigra*) and some grasses release growth-inhibiting compounds as competitive attacks on plants in their immediate environment. These natural herbicides suppress rival plant growth as part of a sophisticated plot to maximize resources and preserve their niche. Chemicals, both organic and synthesized, are insidious in the natural world.

Gardeners fertilize plants as a benevolent gesture, a hope for botanical flourishing. However, both organic and inorganic fertilizers are generally indiscriminate in action. The addition of fertilizers on many soils often encourages weeds and disrupts endemic microbial ecology. The legacies of historic fertilizing can linger for decades, most often echoed by novel plant species or whole communities that continue to subsist on nitrogen-, potassium-, and phosphorus-rich memories. Your grandmother's benevolence is your burden. On severely degraded sites with limited biological activity in the soil, such as you may encounter in post-agricultural and industrial land use, one-time applications may hasten the establishment of desirable plant communities, but these situations are probably the exception for most home gardeners. Feed your houseplants, as you must, but leave nature to tend those outdoors.

In the ongoing life of a natural gardener, there's little reason to employ pesticides when patience will do instead. In my own work, I make an exception only for targeted herbicide applications to arrest existing turf for new plantings. Given that most turf has been chemically managed for some or all of its life, an acutely terminal herbicide application doesn't count, in my mind, as a mortal sin. While the work could happen without it, the results wouldn't happen with the expediency that many clients or stakeholders expect. When patience is in limited supply at the outset, I reason that it's better to cultivate it over the long life of a verdant, ecologically vibrant garden once a gardener has some inkling of initial satisfaction. If you lack such complications of human psychology, count your blessings and continue unheeded.

Many restoration ecologists throw in their lot with herbicides given the scale of their challenges in "combatting" or "warring" with "alien" and "invasive" species. The results speak volumes, even if the threats simply shift on the horizon. While justifying arguments exist for herbicide use at scale, most home gardens are small enough that there's a greater chance the herbicide affects more than what it targets. While labels advise on safety and precautions, the products available on the market today are vastly more lethal by design. Retail versions of

Lawn weeds might prove useful if you know what they are and where they call home, as in the case of the cosmopolitan Prunella vulgaris *(self-heal).*

otherwise commercial pesticides are sold at the hardware store without the same precautions mandated to professionals. These pesticides are tools of efficiency and accomplish their objectives with remarkable efficacy. (As revealing is how readily military vocabulary enters the lexicon when undesirable actors enter the scene. How do plants and bugs trigger such emotions and the need to control our environment?)

Insects, lately, have enjoyed more favorable headlines. The plight of pollinators and the general decline of insect abundance have made international headlines, entering mainstream conversations and even politics. Over the last twenty-five years, inroads with organic agriculture have yielded public-facing messages about "beneficial insects" and the cooperative value of working alongside those creatures already living in our gardens. The phrase amounts to savvy marketing, a moniker designed to shift public perception from entomological aversion towards acceptance. Many books on the subject emphasize the positive impact certain insects have on gardens, farms, and ecosystems, highlighting their roles in pollination and regulating biodiversity.

Insects are now allies in categorical terms, even if we only like some of them (butterflies are in; wasps are still out). Rather than a military approach towards those we don't like, why not adopt words from diplomacy like avoidance and deterrence? In reality, most organisms that threaten something in our gardens aren't permanent, and eradicating them would be futile if not borderline impossible. We want to avoid the worst interactions, deter the bad actors, and aim for an armistice.

A Timely Disturbance

In ecology, disturbances shape ecosystems, even those created by humans, while acting on individuals. Disturbance interrupts or destroys the biomass of an individual plant, which when scaled to the level of a community or ecosystem, can disrupt normal functions or composition, often leading to changes in the abundance and distribution of species. Ultimately, the study of disturbance is the study of change. Disturbance powers the garden, just as it drives ecosystems; planting and gardening introduce new species and control the composition of the garden.

Disturbance can result in thoughtful, concerted interventions with place. To better understand its impacts, it's helpful to consider how the landscape around us may have once been disturbed. Did megafauna shape the distribution of vegetation? Did Indigenous people manage the landscape with acts of agroecology? In contemporary terms, what kind of disturbance are you? Are you an ant? A pocket gopher? A buffalo? Each creature leaves a trace in proportion to its size, no less consequential. Humans have long been agents of ecological disturbance. The present question is what kind of disturbance we wish to create as we chart a new course for living with the landscapes we call home.

Understanding when disturbances naturally occur informs how you might invoke them in your natural garden. Disturbance is agnostic, a fortune that favors the bold. It works to benefit any plant that seizes the opportunity to grow in its wake. The timing of disturbance in the natural garden can magnify or diminish its outcomes. For example, if plants in your bioregion and climate have adapted to grazing at a particular time of year, adopting that schedule makes sense if you have many of those same species in your plantings. In another view, the timing of the disturbance is informed by the timing of the response—can plants regenerate due to having their biomass disturbed, or if not, can they enter dormancy until favorable conditions exist again? The genus *Clematis* is the classic horticultural example of plants that have evolved distinct responses—which gardeners call "pruning groups"—to disturbance based on their origins.

Plant communities respond to disturbance differently based on their composition and growing conditions. Some communities rely on their founders' legacies, resulting from various competitive relationships among colonial, well-adapted species. A founder-controlled community emerges as each new species competes with the founder to establish in the wake of disturbance as the victor. In another scenario, differences in competitiveness yield a predictable sequence of species colonizing an area first. Early species are good colonizers and fast growers. Later species lurk in the shadows, slowly establishing and eventually outcompeting the early species. This pattern mirrors traditional succession, a continuous pattern of colonization and extinction by species' populations on a site.

These patterns happen in garden settings when regular gardening doesn't arrest them. Paradoxically, routine horticulture often battles plant growth. Abundance is the mothering force of ecology, a flourish set in motion by marginal acts of disturbance. But disturbance isn't equal. In some cases, we encourage it. In others, we manage it or even mitigate its effects.

Disturbance happens—let plants quickly repair it. Many rare plants worldwide once thrived in the ripple effects of disturbance from falling trees, seasonal grazing, fire, or not so long ago, railroads. But as conservation focuses so intently on preserving intact areas, ragged edges become afterthoughts. Every garden has a raw edge, some nether region where plant life runs beyond the leash, chasing after the prospect of untamed life. Whether by design or chance, these raw edges offer endless possibilities for working with the self-organizing spirit inherent to every place. Disturbance has a place in your natural garden—cause a judicious ruckus.

This remnant sand prairie in rural Iowa, only briefly used for agriculture decades ago, illustrates the abundance that thrives in the wake of disturbance.

Early colonizers like this Geum macrophyllum *(yellow avens) only thrive for a few years in one place, traveling around the garden over time as canopies close on their first homes and disturbances unearth their seeds in new ones.*

Legibility

"Gardening is a property of living systems: of the garden and of the gardener. It is as elusive to define as life itself. ... A garden cannot function without committed human participation."

—Geoffrey Dutton in *Some Branch Against the Sky*

The concept of legibility is the alter ego of complexity. You could think of it as a tool for addressing a beautiful conundrum: how do you relate dense and diverse plantings to human users? If you garden in the middle of nowhere without neighbors, your standards might look entirely different than someone stewarding ecology along a row of brownstones. While wild gardens are inherently complex, brimming with life and humming with details, many people need cues to understand them. How do we make sense of a garden grown less for its prettiness and more for its abundance? How do we shape color, texture, and form inside looser contexts? Could the natural garden present a new medium of expression, a celebration of place and nature and our relationship to it? If beauty is defined by the pleasure of perception, we should give ourselves more latitude to perceive.

Curiously, then, natural gardening is a performance art in defining limits, a set of methods for intervening with abundance even as it flourishes. These actions work aesthetically on the biological properties of plants, principally by disturbing growth, both of desired and undesirable plants. This interplay between humans and plants operates in the realm of perception. Whether we value it or not, what we see reflects place and the responses of plants to their environment. More than controlling anything, natural gardening is an art of observation and thoughtful response.

By all accounts, this isn't a design chapter. Beyond legibility, a dozen other aesthetic principles could further clarify the natural aesthetic. But let's assume from the outset that cultivating a natural garden in the spirit of place requires ongoing design through stewardship, the kind of balls-and-strikes adjudication that comes with everyday gardening. Some days are for weeding, others are for planting, and so on. Design doesn't cease after planting. It's a recursive and ongoing process—one in which you will change and grow, too.

Situated in a sixth-story courtyard of condos and apartments atop the Barbican Centre (London, UK), this landscape thrives in the steppe-like environment of an exposed roof with moxie and horticultural flair. Design by Nigel Dunnett.

Aesthetics, Pleasure, and Experience

As humans, our perception of the environment informs our experience with it. This emotional interaction leads to subjective evaluations and judgments about the landscape and the development of our aesthetic vocabularies. This perceptible realm—the home of favorite flowers, seasonal color palettes, and textures—is where humans intentionally and directly alter the landscape.

Even for the most conservation-hearted among us, how a landscape looks directly affects how we feel about it. Our perceptions of wilder landscapes have deep roots in our personal experiences, including cultural traditions; where some see nature, others can see neglect and in either view, with very little nuance. Further, across all types of landscapes and people, research illustrates that we aesthetically interpret our surroundings as a proxy for ecological quality. If we find something beautiful, we associate it with being "good" or "high quality," even when it's not. The reverse is also true, suggesting we have hardwired associations of disorder and messiness with fear and contempt. Given this, is it any wonder why gardens or landscapes are often only appraised for their visual beauty at the expense of how they make us feel or how much life they support?

This bane of beauty strikes at a central challenge for planting the world a rich, vibrant place. Without an aesthetic language, it's difficult for people to comprehend, care about, and act upon phenomena that occur beyond their direct experiences. Context affects the aesthetic experience. The natural aesthetic you cultivate in your garden will inherently reflect your values about living there. When you prioritize a stately tree canopy or views of a landform or body of water, you're making an aesthetic judgment about your relationship with the landscape. These judgments could be cultural, too, if your ancestors had a connection to the land you wish to honor or remember. If you're like me, you may have fallen further in love with your place by gardening, an emotional stewardship that's good for mental health. Landscapes can change people just as people change landscapes.

As you grow into your natural garden, challenge yourself to ground your aesthetic experience in ecological awareness. This doesn't require a diet. If anything, you'll keep planting. Curiously, many studies have found that humans like species-rich landscapes. The richness of such landscapes stimulates pleasure and satisfaction, leading viewers to believe that such places are more natural or hospitable to a greater range of creatures. Visual evenness—the balance and harmony of all perceivable species in planting—appeals to people, too. Your natural aesthetic results from those feelings of pleasure inspired by the place you live.

As natural as they can be by design, gardens still exist in a human cultural context. Beauty is subjective but a necessary tool for cultivating deeper relationships with landscapes. Design by Kelly Norris.

Five Ways to Develop Your Natural Style

Cultivating this connection between environment and home, shortening the intellectual distance between ecological restoration and home horticulture, offers anyone a method for engaging with the natural world. The options for creative gardening abound.

- **Discover your nterests.** Gardening is full of experiences defined by plants and the life they support. Do you like floral abundance? Maybe you're drawn to seed heads or other textural, botanical structures. Perhaps you're indifferent to colors and want to plant to encourage wildlife. Whatever your prompt, act confidently. You somehow managed to get dressed this morning; you can find your way into a natural gardening style. If you find yourself drawn to an assorted set of (too many) inspirations, consider your primary motivations first. Plants are always multi-dimensional.

- **Translate, don't copy.** The internet makes finding inspiration easy. But don't simply copy an idea or a plant palette without understanding its context. Borrow the feature that inspires you and translate it into plants for your place.

- **Experiment on a small scale first.** While boldness has merits, you can build confidence in miniatures. You could establish your own trial block (e.g., 10 x 10 feet [3 x 3 m]) to learn how plants perform and study their interactions or repurpose an existing garden bed by simply supplanting it with additional species.

- **Repeat, repeat, repeat.** Practice makes permanent, or so my music teachers always said. Once you get the hang of something, riff a little. Take the recipe and change up the ingredients. This is easy enough to do with colors, textures, and forms. Ecologically, you can dig deeper into the groups of plants that already work or that diversify the plant palette. Maybe you like little details or creating garden environments that slow your pace. You could plant more ephemerals or species with abbreviated bloom times that may offer critical resources to pollinators. These well-timed, if fleeting, events accent the rhythm of the seasons.

- **Don't underestimate your efforts or the time it takes for an idea to develop.** Plantings, unlike a weekend craft project, take time to establish. They're never "finished." Throughout the journey, your ideas will probably evolve. Lean into the process and learn from the experience.

Test your ideas on a small scale first. Start with combinations of three to five species, considering how they change through the seasons. Once you see what works, you can vary the theme.

The Art of Natural Gardening

"As far as aesthetic arts are concerned, gardening is messy. It is fraught with unpredictability, and it is never complete."
—G. R. F. Ferrari

In oft-told fables of gardening, two characters frequently come to loggerheads: the gardener and the designer. The ever-exuberant and unbounded gardener is only interested in plants. They walk the garden daily, marking the passage of time with the comings and goings of the plants in their stead. The designer, visionary and shrewd, maintains a deep commitment to "the vision" as a captain steering a ship towards a yawning horizon. There are rules to abide and lines to respect.

Perhaps we could do with fewer dichotomies, but I proffer to make a point. Both characters have consequential roles to play in a natural garden; indeed, most of us garden on some spectrum between them already. The gardener is the harbinger of plants and more plants, an engine of boundless abundance. The designer's shrewd eye shapes the abundance into a form that impacts how people experience the garden. In a seminal essay, "Messy Ecosystems, Orderly Frames," landscape architect and scholar Joan Nassauer calls these orderly frames. She argued that ecological quality, which can often appear disorderly, poses challenges for those who create new landscapes to enhance it. Translating ecological patterns into cultural language requires a clear and concerted approach to communicating new ways of living with nature.

Design Through Stewardship

Plant-driven gardens unfold with cinematic brilliance, the product of decisions about how they grow. The measurement of a garden's value requires time as a denominator. Your best ideas only start with the design process; they evolve with gardening through the dimension of time. Most aesthetic values are short-term affairs: color, texture, form, and all the sound principles of design you may already know. While some traits are more enduring than others, few plants remain the same throughout their life. As you learn from plantings, you can celebrate long-term plant performance by balancing ecological habits with aesthetic experience. In whatever way the garden changes, keep it lively and in motion.

A natural garden presents an entirely new medium of horticultural expression that lives within the frame but pushes its boundaries. A natural garden offers endless avenues for creative exploration, including liberating your self-consciousness. The garden, as a fluid form, remains receptive, not stilted. It isn't just a place to keep tidy. It's a place for deep sensory engagement, open to all the possibilities unearthed in collaboration with plants, even if this doesn't amount to a blank check. Gardening implies engagement, not capitulation.

As you garden, you will reconcile the lives of plants with how people perceive and value them. If we want to shift our view about the role gardens play, we should consider an aesthetic vocabulary that allows beauty and ecology to thrive in unison. Designing through stewardship enhances the aesthetic experience alongside the growth of the garden. Through stewardship, we rearrange and reprioritize, even as plants grow. The art of natural gardening is defined by how you shape the aesthetic experience without compromising the functional value of the garden ecosystem.

Stagecraft in planting design involves a bit of botanical rigging. The soft, airy form of Panicum *'Bad Hair Day' (Bad Hair Day switchgrass) sets the stage for* Rudbeckia subtomentosa *'Henry Eilers' (Henry Eilers sweet coneflower).* Carex muskingumensis *(palm sedge) plays the role of understory matrix.*

A large slope confronts visitors to a performing arts venue, a powerful feeling of being immersed in landscape. Imagine the impact on public life if more landscapes grew like this. Planting design by Kelly Norris, Simpson College (Indianola, Iowa, US).

Once More with Feeling

We experience landscapes across various emotions, from excitement and elation to serenity and tranquility. As plantings evolve, so will your feelings about them. Research from the University of Sheffield shows that attractive plantings trigger excitement and arousal, particularly when flower coverage exceeds 27 percent of the land surface. Studies of human evolution explain our appreciation of colorful flowers as cues to our survival. Flowers suggest abundance, both naturally and as a cultural fingerprint of human intentions. You can leverage this innate benchmark in your gardening: do you have enough flowers to stimulate your interests and support the pollinators that rely on them? But flowers aren't always everywhere, particularly in places where resources may only support flowers in particular seasons. The shady calm of woodland in summer has rejuvenating effects on the human condition but occurs because the resource of light is maximal in spring and, to a limited extent, in fall. No amount of planting will resiliently re-engineer this circumstance; plants aren't machines. While colorful flowering plants are exciting, embrace greenery as a necessary counterpoint. Aesthetics and ecology can go hand in hand.

Color isn't the only feature of plants that stimulates the senses. The vegetation structure leads our eyes to perceive patterns and forms, organizing elements that help our brains process the scene and assess our comfort. Foliage and the structures of plants endure for most of the growing season—how do you contend with their endurance? In the same study from the University of Sheffield, plantings with a moderate or highly natural structure were perceived as significantly more restorative than those with more contrived planting styles. In their way, the data suggests we should loosen up. Naturalness and order are not mutually exclusive.

Soft Focus

In aesthetic theory, coherency refers to the unity and harmony within a design, where every element feels like an integral part of the whole. Conversely, legibility pertains to the clarity and ease with which an observer can understand and interpret the design. A coherent design ensures that all components work together seamlessly, while a legible design ensures that the viewer can readily grasp the intent and structure of the composition. Both are crucial in creating spaces that are not only visually appealing but also meaningful and accessible.

When I think about planting, I want to capture the essence of the place that's unique. Disentangling what you see and what it means takes practice, particularly in the company of many different plant species. I always ask, "What makes *here* look different than *there*?" Having spent considerable time in natural plant communities, I'm inspired by the atmospheres of these places. The life of each plant contributes to this intangible sense of place deeply rooted in plant growth. In my gardens, I like to plant for clarity but only modest precision (plants don't always stay where you put them, after all). As in photography, keeping the focus soft produces a gentle, dreamy quality. It unravels complexity and amplifies the mood. In research on aesthetics and landscape psychology, the human appetite for complexity is defined by the sub-

Some plants—like Oenothera gaura *(biennial gaura)— earn the adjective "atmospheric" when they seem to convey an ambient lightness, floating through the garden as if carried on the wind.*

jective bounds of too much and too little; Goldilocks had it right. With too much complexity, our minds shudder with incomprehension. With too little complexity, we're simply bored. While complexity can work against legibility, it only succeeds when the standard for clarity is rigid and precise. Every plant doesn't need to be in focus in a natural garden; the components work additively but not always equally.

Some plants land an opportunity to sprout and put down deep roots to stay, like this Euphorbia corollata *(flowering spurge)* that brings a scintillating cloud of white flowers to this meadow vignette.

Drama

Like a good film, gardens offer endless drama across a broad spectrum of emotions and experiences. This liveliness is what lures us. Drama calls up a range of creative devices from the whole of human art, contrast most of all. Contrasting elements vary the value and magnitude of different properties within the garden, adding depth and interest to the composition. In small gardens, every plant matters, influencing the garden's overall aesthetic and functional coherence. As plants thrive and perish in your natural garden, consider how changes affect the garden's rhythm, cadence, and tempo. Does a new addition (or deletion, for that matter) enhance or muddy the pattern? As you assess your plantings, increase the drama by doing the following:

- For more sociable plants, maximize their impact by planting larger groupings of them. While you may have started with three or five individuals, consider increasing each grouping to nine or more. Prominent statements improve legibility by underscoring the idea.

- Repeat features of plants, even if those features appear in more than one species. A diverse meadow features many species doing similar things (ecologically and aesthetically). Consider how wind moves through grasses. Thoughtful layering of a few species produces subtle themes and romantic variations.

- Consider a well-placed contradiction. Patterns can become too predictable. Even as you work to cultivate rhythm and unity across your landscape, don't forego the opportunity for something unique. In nature, you'll readily encounter species of rarer abundance, represented by only one or a few individuals. These treasured encounters in a garden setting deepen the atmosphere and inspire curiosity. How did this get here? Why is there only one? If it stops you on a stroll through the garden, as it would if you stumbled upon it in nature, make it worth the stop.

Making livable landscapes is an art of transition. Transitions between spaces heighten anticipation, inspiring movement and curiosity at what grows beyond this well-planted interruption in a wall at Great Dixter (UK).

Good Bones

Wilder planting schemes require some structure the closer they live to the human experience. This includes and goes beyond the more oversized frame espoused by Nassauer and described in the previous essay. The frame can be a fence, a significant object, or a mowed path. But inside the picture, plants should lean on each other in partnership for a coherent view. Structural plants—typically trees, shrubs, and coarsely formed herbaceous perennials—are the good bones of your natural garden.

Structural plants often give the first clues as the age of a garden, the most likely surface to interpret the patina of time. Contending with the constancy of growth means that plants aren't architectural unless the definition of architecture is secondary to unlimited growth. The garden's bones succeed in shorter time scales when viewers can perceive biodiverse vegetation as an intentional if also beautiful, habitat. These good bones define spaces, bring form to the formless, and create corridors for wildlife to venture in and call home.

Structure in Time and Space

Unless you begin with an established canopy, hedge, or existing shrubs, the evolution of structure in your garden starts after you conclude planting. A tree planted as a seedling might trace a long arc from sapling to maturity and not have much "structural" value until years later. While I'm not necessarily advocating for planting large trees out of impatience, you should consider the shoulders upon which you place the burden of structure. If you've planted small trees with hope and patience, you may want to lean on a coarse perennial to fill the short-term void. Apart from anything else you grow, structural plants are intimately linked with the passage of time.

Structure may come in different forms depending on your geography and your established plant communities. Technically speaking, form is often described as the overall shape of a woody plant as defined by its branches and trunk from the ground to the limits of its growth in mid-air. You can get lost for an afternoon in a park, doodling the shapes of trees and shrubs as you encounter them, a valuable exercise for understanding form as design vocabulary. But putting form to use requires animating it in space. How do long-lived, perennial plants relate to one another?

Most residential gardens grow beneath canopies, leading to a more intimate consideration of structure. Here are some general terms you can consider as you study and evaluate plantings for their structural significance.

- **Foil**—A plant with subdued features that emphasizes a more striking neighbor, enhancing its colors, shapes, or textures and drawing attention to specific features by comparison. Grassland environments, in particular, feature many species that serve as visual foils to others, not the least of which are the grasses. Using grasses in structural roles makes sense so long as they remain clumped and discrete in habit; rhizomatous species wouldn't accomplish the same effect.

- **Scaffold**—A series of plants that form a visual framework for spatially organizing plantings, generally of the same visual weight if not the same species. Think of plants in this role as necessary visual infrastructure, additions to enhance the legibility of a planting.

- **Scrim and Veil**—Plants with tailored architecture or fine-textured habits that achieve prominence when backlit or illuminated to the visual benefit of nearby plants. I use this term interchangeably for species in various layers of the landscape. Still, some plants with prominent seasonal floral displays atop towering proportions (e.g., tall herbaceous perennials or small to medium trees) deserve their own descriptor. Their structural contributions may be briefer but no less critical.

A foil for most of the growing year, tall evergreens like Thuja occidentalis *(arborvitae) regain prominence as pillars of the planting in autumn and winter.*

The *Juniperus virginiana 'Taylor' (Taylor eastern red cedar)* scaffold this fine-textured, small-flowered translation of sand prairie.

Salvia reptans *(West Texas sage)* benefits from the scrim of Muhlenbergia reverchonii *'PUND01S'* *(UNDAUNTED® muhly grass), an effect most dramatically achieved when backlit.*

Desire Lines

How you move through your garden defines your perception of it. While an initial design often lays out paths and defines areas for planting, you may find a reason to move elsewhere as your landscape matures. A canopy offers a welcome respite from hot summer days and a new opportunity to see the garden. Some plants might tower above you, perfect for ducking under as if reclaiming the playfulness of your youth. Maybe as you age, you'll want more details closer to the house. Desire lines also develop naturally as we invent new ways of traveling between two points, perhaps iconically defined as the shortest path between two buildings on a college campus, whether or not a sidewalk exists. Users of a space often define their own experience. Regardless of the change, your movements define your collisions with nature. As the poet Wendell Berry wrote:

> A path is little more than a habit that comes with knowledge of a place. It is a sort of ritual of familiarity. As a form, it is a form of contact with a known landscape. It is not destructive. It is the perfect adaptation, through experience and familiarity, of movement to place; it obeys the natural contours; such obstacles as it meets, it goes around.

The late Dutch plantsman and designer Henk Gerritsen offered a helpful axiom for evaluating lines in landscapes: what is curved should be straight, and what is straight should be curved. How a path intersects space has ecological and aesthetic implications but requires some appreciation of the size of your lot or landscape and its existing dimensions. Ecologically, it's essential to preserve as much core area space as possible to minimize the net impact of disturbance as received from the edge. Park designers have used these ideas for decades to devise where trails should and shouldn't go. Smaller beds in your garden will almost always warrant more attention than larger ones simply because they are more disturbed. While some disturbance is good, needless mucking around only serves up more problems.

Aesthetically, paths and lines of sight through the garden help to convey a sense of safety and security. Research shows that people can feel overwhelmed easily by natural-like vegetation unless given ample views through it. This is especially true in small gardens because, as your garden grows, your relationship to the scale of vegetation changes quickly. Former good proportions can easily give way to clutter and awkwardness. Managing trees and shrubs accordingly can achieve optimal ratios of canopy to understory while preserving viewing portals into the landscape.

The gentle curving path through our front yard Meadow Nord at Three Oaks Garden (Des Moines, Iowa, US) connects to distant sight lines that invite movement through the space.

Before coppicing.

Pruning

Contending with plant growth occupies much gardening attention, especially with trees and shrubs. Pruning is a craft of observation informed by the predictability and unpredictability of otherwise sedentary organisms. Volumes exist on the proper pruning cuts and when to make them for a wide berth of species. The commentary here focuses primarily on evaluating and undertaking pruning from the perspective of promoting life and its movements in the garden environment.

Ecologically inspired pruning focuses on promoting plants' natural shape and health while minimizing disturbance to the community. Depending on your landscape, you may undertake these efforts at various scales—from second-growth forests to windbreaks and hedgerows. Habitat pruning creates spaces for wildlife by removing branches to enhance sunlight penetration and air circulation. It also prioritizes leaving remnant mature trees and decaying snags so long as they don't threaten human safety.

Pruning, as an act of disturbance, increases light to the understory, releasing species below it from competition. As canopies redevelop, you will strike a balance between various age classes of trees and shrubs to maximize habitat quality, complexity, and structure. Ideally, you want to maximize the amount of edge area. Meandering boundaries enhance habitat diversity by creating a mosaic of niches that favors more species. Plan for how the

After coppicing. Growth will resprout from crown tissue just below the line of cuts, producing rampant juvenile growth until cut again the following year.

canopy transitions into open space, especially in a hedgerow setting where shrubs and trees of various sizes are growing densely. As you make cuts, conserve the debris as a habitat for various plants, animals, and insects while contributing to soil development as it decomposes. Pile logs and larger, coarse materials for wildlife cover, artful boundaries (like a log pile fence), or unique garden rooms (like a stumpery). Make it look done but not dead. Sticks are life.

Rejuvenative pruning, such as coppicing, revitalizes older plants by cutting them back significantly to encourage new growth, mimicking natural events —namely fire, grazing, and flooding. Early successional species— members of the birch and willow families, for instance—adapt well to this treatment and may disappear in time without it. Coppicing is an early form of agroecological forestry, an ancient practice for managing woodland environments for productive harvesting that yields valuable wildlife habitat in the wake of disturbance.

Structural pruning, the kind of pruning intervention practiced most often in traditional horticulture, reduces canopy biomass for the benefit of long-term architectural integrity. However, ecologically speaking, these activities reduce habitats for canopy-residing birds and invertebrates, especially spiders, though usually only in the short term. The trade-offs for short-term habitat loss rarely win over the long-term priority of the tree's life. With each passing year, a mature tree offers a compounding rate of ecological return. Its biomass pays dividends.

As diversity increases, patterns become more complex. This planting pattern features color and texture in complementary strokes (like warp and weft), relying on ample silver and blue offset by staccato strokes of orange and yellow. Planting design by Jonathan Wright, Chanticleer Garden (Wayne, Pennsylvania, US).

Patterns

Patterns power process. Natural gardens aren't bespoke combinations of prized specimens but evolving cohorts that vary in patterns across large and small spaces. Designed plant communities based on natural patterns marry ecological principles with aesthetic values, translating rhythm and movement into garden-scale forms. As plant communities settle into place, they generate a mass of raw material to work from, a sheer abundance that produces the plant-driven experience of a natural garden.

By definition, an effective pattern is visually appealing and harmonious, balancing repetition and variation to engage the viewer. A pattern-based approach is more spatial, spreading aesthetics over a visual surface bigger than a plant combination of a few species tucked into one corner of the garden. While every species can't be everywhere simultaneously, in a residential setting, you should attempt to balance diversity with cohesion. Beautiful patterns are founded on proportion, scale, and spacing, ensuring a coherent and aesthetically pleasing result. Curiously, the same elements also apply when evaluating ecologically stable patterns. Planting patterns can be achieved both with some due consideration and good gardening.

Set the Pattern, Then Break It

When you commence planting, you should establish regular, predictable patterns that form the basis of your design and its durable assumptions. These initial patterns may come from wild plant communities and generally start with a dominant element, often abundant and scattered, followed by layering additional components in

Visual evenness belies ecological reality—despite appearing to be a monoculture of Eschscholzia californica *(California poppy), this Mojave Desert plant community supports dozens of other species, just at lower levels of abundance. In your garden, lean on one or a few species to visually carry each season.*

diminishing abundance. This approach mirrors natural patterns, such as the Fibonacci sequence, which can serve as valuable prompts for scaling plants in relationship to each other (provided they grow at the level of social abundance you assign them). Adopting the pattern approach ensures a commitment to cohesion; if one or two elements falter, it's easier to identify and resolve.

After a few initial seasons, your durable assumptions may have thrived beyond recognition or stumbled through the first season. In the former situation, stick to the plan. This is the hardest part. A reasonable gardener thinks, "What if things get out of control?" A natural gardener thinks, "What if plants exceed all expectations?" Of course, if your assumptions prove fragile, enjoy being wrong and then learn from it. What lived? What didn't? How did they grow? Were resources limited, or did plants not perform as expected? Planting patterns are often easily mended or augmented, but not without understanding why your assumptions faltered. Try to resist dogmatic conclusions.

As designed plant communities grow and develop with time, you should strive to preserve their visual integrity, especially as it varies across the landscape. But to keep things consistent, you may have to shift your approach. Natural plant communities fluctuate wildly in abundance from year to year based on weather, chance, and many other acts of nature. Some species may take years to establish at an appreciable level. Your job is to keep the party going, even as plants fade in and out of the scene.

Evenness

Designing plant communities involves a thoughtful balance of evenness and diversity. Evenness, a concept from scientific literature, gauges how plant mass is

distributed among species, informed by plant sociality and depicted as aesthetic patterns. This approach aims for a landscape where a few dominant species harmoniously coexist with a diverse range of others, creating a visually coherent and ecologically robust environment. Each plant contributes to a balanced, readable garden, which is especially crucial in smaller spaces where every species significantly impacts the overall aesthetic and ecological function. This approach ensures the landscape is visually engaging and ecologically sound, adapting to different gardens' varying scales and contexts.

Applying naturalistic planting concepts to small gardens transcends scale limitations. Many urban gardens showcase dense, diverse plantings, debunking the notion that "natural" requires expansive spaces. In these intimate settings, every plant significantly contributes to the ecosystem. Size constraints, however, influence plant interactions and the garden's visual and ecological outcomes. Thoughtful plant choices and arrangements, acknowledging their life spans and ecological roles, ensure these small gardens remain dynamic, visually appealing, and vibrant. The results meld the novel urban context with a place-based identity that honors natural heritage and contemporary realities.

The primary pattern element in this steppe meadow is Andropogon gerardii *(big bluestem)*, a matrix species that appears with welcome regularity. Planting design by Kevin Philip Williams, SummerHome Garden (Denver, Colorado, US).

What About Color?

"Color surrounds us, often confounds us."
—Nori and Sandra Pope in *Color by Design:*
Planting the Contemporary Garden

Color, color, color. Our brains are wired to notice it, and the subject preoccupies design. I grew up reasonably ambivalent about color, having no strong opinions or preferences that made much of a difference in my life as a gardener. While specific color patterns and themes emerge seasonally in wild plant communities, flower color is merely an artifact of plant reproductive biology that stirs human emotions. Flowers don't exist for our entertainment, even if we enjoy them.

Color has held an outsized and undeniable influence on horticultural attentions for over a century. Nori and Sandra Pope's *Color by Design: Planting the Contemporary Garden* is an enlightened, artistic work on the subject written by two masters of the craft. Their Hadspen Garden in Somerset, England, was a destination for color seekers. Two decades later, many readers might wonder if color has any merits in the discussion of a natural garden. Given the motivation to put plants in the lead, should we indulge the aesthetic whims of a color preference when making a meadow or a hedgerow?

Whether you put color theory to work in your natural garden for ornamental purposes, color also offers an opportunity to engage pollinator diversity with the resources they require to fulfill their lives. Floral traits, known as *pollination syndromes*, have evolved to entice particular pollinators. Pollination syndromes encompass various floral characteristics, including color, shape, size, scent, nectar production, and flower structure. Researchers have questioned the straightforwardness of the issue, as most pollinator groups are generalized foragers that can visit plants with distinct floral phenotypes. These interactions depend on floral traits and which species are present. For example, beetles more readily perceive yellow and white flowers, while flies can differentiate between many colors, differences accounted for based on the structure of their eyes.

Certain floral traits, like floral display area, serve as general signals across different pollinator groups, while others, such as plant height, are more taxon-specific. A taller cultivar, for instance, can expand the pollinator community without excluding other bee taxa; some bees forage at different elevations within a planting. In bees, different floral traits can expand or limit the visiting pollinator community. In studies done at Pennsylvania State University (2022), researchers found that purple-colored cultivars of *Agastache*, *Nepeta*, and *Salvia* attracted many species of bees, while non-purple ones supported only a subset. In each case, purple was the dominant color from natural source populations in each of the genera studied. Bees have color preferences, too.

A sun-washed vignette at Great Dixter (Rye, Sussex, UK) illustrating immense details in an immersive space. Note the well-played Consolida regalis *(larkspur), romping through a green and yellow scene.*

Nature Is More Colorful Than You Think

I embrace the distraction of color, especially when natural plant palettes offer ample choices. While you may not *make* a natural garden with color in mind, including color patterns and combinations conveys an aesthetic narrative that catches the eye. Someone passing your front yard may not know a plant's name, but its flower color could be the introduction to more profound curiosity.

Despite aesthetic appraisals to the contrary, naturalistic plant palettes don't have to be boring, subdued exercises in tonality (although tonal color blends offer endless possibilities). Bold, jarring colors exist in many natural color palettes, often when we don't expect them. Consider the arresting pigments produced in flowers of the genus *Rhododendron*, ranging from the sunshine warmth of *R. calendulaceum* (flame azalea) to the plush pink of *R. sutchuenense* (Sichuan rhododendron). These plants come from places where color leaps from dark understories, reflecting light into visual space. In context, there is value in standing out from the crowd. Garden-making in the spirit of place should honor the personalities of plants that convey and define it. In every biome or ecoregion, indigenous plant communities and even those of recently established plants define an aesthetic vocabulary that our brains associate with geography.

Rhododendron austrinum (Florida azalea) flickers in brilliant contradiction to an otherwise green scene in the understory of Louise Agee Wrinkle's acclaimed southern woodland garden (Birmingham, Alabama, US).

In a northern temperate climate in late autumn,
flower color is a gift and a resource, as here with
Symphyotrichum oblongifolium *'Raydon's
Favorite'* (Raydon's Favorite aromatic aster).

Planting Amid Existing Vegetation

If you readily adopt the motto "just keep planting," at some point, you will encounter the chore of emplacing new plants alongside existing ones. There are at least a thousand good reasons for adding to an established landscape motivated by everything from preference to prescription. You may want to cultivate as much diversity as possible (a preference). You may desire to amplify an existing planting towards a greater regional identity that often includes native species naturally occurring at low abundance levels (a prescription). Midway through this activity, you may question your objectives or sanity. Wouldn't it be better to leave this all undisturbed? But with a gardener's persistence, you'll likely keep on as you've made it this far already.

If you need to kill existing vegetation, do so as lightly as possible. If the vegetation is indigenous to the site and beyond the realm of recent gardening, consider how you might embrace it rather than erase it. While a gentle approach is often desirable, it's also not always realistic. Suppose the species you remove have outgrown their station. In that case, this may be a worthwhile and liberating act, particularly if it results in an additional, valuable species you previously weren't cultivating. What is most important when replacing something is not how you remove it but what you put in its place. All planting is a form of ecological disturbance and, for all its merits, can often yield ripple effects that linger long after you've hung up the trowel. Don't simply avoid disturbance, but consider the implications.

As with establishing a new planting wholesale, avoid tillage as much as possible. While freshly tilled soil feeds an agronomic instinct of speed and ease, it's unnecessarily disruptive to soil microorganisms and the physical structure of the soil column. If you're

The motto "just keep planting" leads you to place new young plants within established garden areas, which requires careful thought regarding plant size and timing.

Even more "traditional" gardens can grow into a more natural spirit. This amplified border planting brims with self-sowers and competitive perennials, remaining complex and resourceful for abundant insects. Planting design by Kelly Norris, Bailey Nursery Display Garden (Cottage Grove, Minnesota, US).

planting in a tight niche, any tillage will disrupt nearby root systems, which may have adverse effects.

Consider the size of what you're planting. Tucking in a plug beneath a large established perennial with a heavy foliar canopy will only succeed if the new-comer gets enough water initially. You may want to "size up" the competition, so to speak, and consider new plants at similar sizes to those preexisting. The timing of planting matters, too. Spring and autumn are more generous starting lines for recruits.

Your sensitivity to how much water your soil holds is the first instinct to cultivate as a gardener. As obvi-ous as it is to write, plant into the rain. Sometimes, life gets in the way, but planting into the rain makes good sense, especially when considering tap water versus rainwater chemistry. After the rain, consider when to water again. You may forego watering in heavy or medium-textured soils post-deluge

for a few days. If you received less than an inch (2.5 cm) of precipitation, you may soon need to water, and then you should do so deeply. Repeat infrequently. The volume of water required by new plantings (both as individuals and as a system) can't be overstated. In an existing system, the answer is more nuanced as the canopy of adjacent plants helps conserve water by modulating evapotranspiration and relative humidity close to the ground. The canopy can also restrict the volume of water received by young plants lurking in their shadows. There are few instances where "plant and forget" makes sense, but they exist, especially when working with miner-al-based media like pea gravel, sand, or recycled hard materials. Initial deep watering is critical.

Naturalizing the Traditional Border

Managing cultivated naturalistic gardens involves embracing disturbance to enhance planting diversity and complexity. Most borders began as ornamental exercises, and because of that, often support a diverse cast of perennial species. There are worse starting points. As you undertake enhancement, consider the balance between plant diversity and visual appeal. Be mindful of the competitive nature of existing species (intentional and undesired) that might dominate the space if given additional room to flourish.

In crafting a cultivated naturalistic garden, it's essential to strategically use the three layers—matrix, structure, and vignettes—to captivate interest throughout the seasons. The matrix layer is often missing from traditional borders because it was supplanted with mulch instead. Accessorizing this layer delivers immediate practical benefits by introducing a few species as "green mulch." A well-chosen, shade-tolerant palette avoids cluttering the border's aesthetic.

The structural layer of border plantings often stay—why arrest and disturb the growth of established plants unless they threaten the ecology of the new space? Even well-intentioned replanting can introduce more disturbance than it's worth, even in a small space. If you're hell-bent on removing something, do so with well-reasoned intentions after considering the merits of existing plant life.

The vignettes of an existing border were likely the reason you made that garden in the first place. As you edit these for aesthetic and ecological clarity, ensure the spring layer blends seamlessly into the background as seasons progress. Many cool-season perennials enter dormancy just in time for this successional handoff. But for those with persistent structures, plan for them in the design or choose wisely. Regardless of seasonality, avoid highly competitive plants that may overwhelm the garden's diversity or, in general, match the sociality of pairwise plant groups to facilitate more even competition. As gaps remain, fill them with ruderal serendipitous species that can move and travel with the seasons. Even if the border becomes a campy version of a local ecological precedent, it's still more diverse and resourceful than the parking lot down the street.

The Long Border at Great Dixter is an ongoing production in horticultural theatre that supports considerable biodiversity as measured in their ecological site surveys. The key is plant diversity and vegetation complexity.

Symphyotrichum pilosum *(frost aster), like many species in its genus, grows more densely and attractively after a midsummer chop. You can trace the dark stems in this photo to the point they were cut, obscured by flowers.*

The Chopping Block

Arresting plant growth is a gardener's judicial action. For some plants, it's revenge served cold. For others, it's more parental, like lopping off a kid's shaggy hair after one too many refusals to visit the barber. In either mindset, the result is the same. Some plants need and have evolved to expect a shearing biomass reduction during the growing season.

Editing the garden like a manuscript is a clarifying exercise with the goal to help someone read and understand what they're seeing. When legibility wobbles, it's time to break out the blades. Horticulturally, cutting back individual plants or populations during the growing season involves temporarily restoring the visual quality of a scene. It helps when editing parts of the garden to have an objective, even a loosely defined rule that benchmarks your actions. You should edit for something, not against it. While the action works on one or a few plant species, you intend for the result to fill the vacuum. (You may break this rule often.)

You arrest growth at this time to promote more growth later. The so-called Chelsea chop, a colloquial term referencing the timing of the activity in British gardening culture as two weeks after the Chelsea Flower Show, reduces apical dominance and stimulates branching. Many late-season perennials in the aster family, such as *Helianthus* (sunflower), *Helenium* (sneezeweed), *Symphyotrichum* (North American aster), and more, respond to this judiciousness with verve. Some warm-season grasses, like species in the genus *Bouteloua* (blue grama) and *Panicum virgatum* (switchgrass), take on new robustness after this grazing by hand.

Grasses native to rangeland ecosystems—like Bouteloua gracilis *(blue grama)—evolved under grazing pressures. Rejuvenating them with occasional midsummer cutting prolongs their life and vibrancy in planting.*

Ecologically, cutting plants back mirrors grazing, imitating disturbance that only temporarily strains its reserves. While I love all forms of grazing (whether by machine, hand, or jowl), tending to plant growth in this way requires knowing which plants don't mind the munch. Deciding which species responds best to this action requires some trial and error. If a plant can't recover from the disturbance in the weeks and months remaining in the growing season, it's probably not a good candidate for chopping back. Additionally, some species may have the energy to recover but may not show well for it. Chopping these plants back produces an awkward, squirrelly profusion of new stems that invites more questions than answers. Previous gardening books illustrate a variety of methods for performing the cuts. These practices have merits as tools of horticultural precision. But even if you aren't skilled in the finer points, give it a try and observe what happens.

Pulling out or cutting back something you've planted is an absolute pleasure. It succeeded beyond your wildest expectations. Reducing mass and restoring legibility is undoubtedly only possible when a garden has grown with abundance. Even happy accidents can shed insights into how plants grow and respond to the nature of place. Some years ago, I had a light-hearted exchange with Maine-based planting designer Caleb Davis that produced a new version we jokingly called the Chelsea trample. I remarked how wonderful it was that he still had *Scutellaria incana* (hoary skullcap) in flower in his garden in September when it peaks typically earlier in the summer. He observed that a few plants were accidentally trampled shortly after planting in late spring but recovered enough to flower, just lagging the rest by several weeks. It was a testament to resilience, a reminder to grow populations of plants that can shoulder disturbance and not take every flower at face value. Some just show up late.

Flow

"Time works at unraveling the design. It outmaneuvers the knowledgeable speculations, the fine anticipations. It transforms certainties into daily questions and knowledge into a mass of data. ...Inert. Turned on their head once exposed. Indispensable and inadequate."

—Gilles Clément in *The Planetary Garden*

Many things flow through the garden. The garden is constantly in motion. Energy moves through the garden in almost infinite directions. The gardener participates in this constant motion, managing energy and how it affects the liveliness of the landscape. The gardener tracks time, mindful of the flow, and what changes.

Time is hard to characterize in natural terms, even as it's easy to lose track of when hunched over a pile of weeds and debris. The impermanence of gardens and the time spent in them calls to mind Carl Sagan's description of Earth as "a mote of dust suspended in a sunbeam." What flows in also flows out. The lively neighbors in our gardenhood pass from one garden to the next, tracing a life between patches of habitat defined by their order. Water drains at the surface and the ground. Plants move upwards and outwards.

Embracing inevitable change requires both conceptual and practical moorings. What tools do you need for gardening differently? What do you weed and how? How do you make space for life moving through the garden? Knowing when to act or intervene stumps even the most astute gardeners. As it should. Methods should be connected to knowledge, observations, or questions. In an ecological garden, questions often guide more activities than confidence does. Your intuition grows with experience based on seasons, weather, plants, and time, rather than a manual prescribing activity under the guise of best practice. As you learn, recipes and formulas are helpful guides, but eventually, the work becomes more instinctual and less dictated by rules. The method for managing your natural garden grows with the flow of life.

As time passes, you may find that some native species come back to your garden on their own. Make space for them as we did in our meadow path for Antennaria plantaginifolia *(plantain pussytoes).*

Succession in the Garden

"One must learn to be satisfied with surprise—and mostly I'm surprised to learn how difficult that is."
—Gilles Clément in *The Planetary Garden*

In his book, *Discovering the Vernacular Landscape*, landscape theorist and author John Brinckerhoff Jackson described landscape as "the field where humans and nature joust for time." The origin of the words "landscape" and "garden" offers an explanation for why gardeners find it difficult to deal with change over time, even as both in their original conceptions were hardly static. "Landscape" referred to scenery, the land that was worth seeing, while "garden" referred to enclosure, vegetation that was guarded and protected. A natural garden challenges the foundations of both. Landscapes are not just scenery, and gardens can be defined by what connects them to the landscape. But seeing and protecting underlie our attitudes about our surroundings. What happens when the nature of a plant, a planting, or a place changes?

Not every plant lives forever. Landscapes shift in structure and composition as plant species shift in abundance and reorder their communities. Ecologists call this process *succession*, a natural phenomenon by which ecosystems change and develop over time. Scientists once saw this process as orderly and predictable in movement towards a final "climax" community that persisted indefinitely. Today, we understand that succession is not linear or predetermined but operates on stable trajectories in local scale environments like gardens, for instance. The patterns we can observe in the garden derive from the diversity of the habitat, which species occur there, and the competition between those plants.

I've always been amused by the relationship between the words success and succession, even as they suggest two incompatible trajectories for the development of a landscape. In terms of the natural garden, a planting *succeeds* by its components *succeeding* into ever different forms in the future. Embracing that dynamic in your natural garden honors the rhythms and complexities of natural systems.

*Plan for changes in the garden by cooperating with both short- and long-lived species (*Elymus hystrix *[bottlebrush grass] and* Carex bicknellii *[Bicknell's sedge], respectively), as here with two graminoids in an oak savanna. Planting design by Kelly Norris.*

Stages of Garden Succession

Successional change is a dynamic process that unfolds gradually and plays a vital role in shaping the character and biodiversity of an ecological garden. Every planting begins with some disturbance, whether as a blank canvas or as an opening in some existing landscape. Succession typically starts with pioneer species—the first plants to colonize the bare ground, ideally those you planted, but also including weeds. These original species pave the way for subsequent changes in the garden's plant community. As the garden progresses from its initial state through later states, complexity and diversity usually increase to the benefit of resilience. The mid-successional stage is characterized by the development of shrubs and small trees to the extent expected in your region. Later successional species including long-lived woody plants and herbaceous perennials, enhance the vertical layering of the garden, deepening the ecological functionality of the place as it approaches its fabled climax. You probably dream of a self-sustaining climax community, a haven for biodiversity akin to undisturbed natural landscapes.

But then something unexpected happens: a tree falls; a drought occurs; or your neighbors start feeding deer, and suddenly, the grazing pressures on your garden increase. Herbivory may not dent a resilient system, but some species might falter. A fallen tree restarts the successional clock if it makes a wholesale change to understory light exposure. A natural gardener, acting as a keystone species, embraces inevitable change, even finding ways to arrest succession if it serves the goal of promoting a diverse, abundant community.

Succession provides a framework for gardeners to influence the complex interactions of life in their gardens. For much of the mid-twentieth century, scientists attempted to model and describe succession as a way of understanding how and why natural plant communities changed. Some versions considered the soil seed bank as a bench full of runners in a race, passing the baton from one cohort of plants to another. Other camps of thought leaned into the idea that individual plants acting on the environment could change the community, facilitating, tolerating, or inhibiting their neighbors. The idea of succession as a process driven by individual species' responses to changing resources encourages a dynamic view of gardening, where change is expected and embraced rather than resisted.

These models highlight the importance of species interactions and life history traits in determining the successional path. Every choice you make at planting may not haunt you forever, but some will persist and shape the evolution of the plant community. The brief chronology of the garden forgives faults and commends good deeds. There is horticultural wisdom in the Jerry Herman lyric "Time heals everything," even if the amount of time required surpasses human understanding.

Succeeding with the Garden

Gardeners play an active role in shaping the successional trajectory of their gardens, contrary to suggestions of a laissez-faire approach. Understanding succession shifts your role from creator to facilitator, embracing change as constant and integral to the nature of place. Through selective planting, managing growth, and enhancing habitat features, gardeners steer succession toward desired ecological outcomes. Gardening becomes part of a constantly evolving ecological story, full of potential for discovery and innovation. The more inflexible your approach, the more resistant nature becomes.

Two photos were taken from a similar position approximately two years apart. Note the increased abundance of Ratibida pinnata *(gray-headed coneflower) and the subtle change in composition around it. The view remains similar, but the components shift.*

Acts of gardening mirror succession, reinforcing and redefining design. The gardener and author James Golden, in his memoir *The View from Federal Twist*, wrote:

> I approached making the garden as an "interweaving" of the new with the old; I was working "at the moment" and was open to new plants seeding in and existing plants moving about. Every act of planting was provisional in nature, subject to change, either intentionally or by some random action.

While sedentary, plants don't always stay exactly where you put them. I embrace movement in almost every way but am mindful of its amplitude and speed. Acting as a keystone species, I can exert some influence on what changes, even as the plantings remain receptive to that beyond my control. Consider three types of natural fluctuations as defined by science—regular (recurrent and predictable), random (impossible to predict), and chaotic (only predictable in the short term and extremely sensitive). I think of regular fluctuations such as mowing, grazing, and even weeding, tasks that readily produce consistent results in a given growing year. Random fluctuations are generally acts of nature, forces we respond to in the natural garden. Pruning, curiously, is an example of chaotic fluctuation. A series of careful pruning cuts often are followed by expected results—buds breaking and new growth—but unknown consequences on longer timelines. I imagine elephants tromping through the African savanna having a similar effect on the structure of canopies.

River Vartry runs through Mount Usher Gardens in County Wicklow, Ireland, previously the site of an ancient lake. The story of the gardens and the river are inseparable.

A Steady Flow

Have you ever considered the resources your garden requires? Water comes to mind first. In a world of extremes, every plant requires water at some point in its life. In wetlands, water is inundating life support. In steppes, where drought tolerance is an asset, plants still require water to establish and reach their full potential. Maybe you also thought of nutrients, which is especially important if you grow food in your natural garden. These critical environmental processes flow through the garden as much as the garden contributes to them. The interconnectedness of individual actions impacts the environment far beyond your backyard fence, with implications for the integrity of rivers, streams, wetlands, and groundwater reserves. As a natural gardener, you should become aware of your garden's resource footprint and how resources linger on the land rather than racing off to somewhere else.

Water

Water is one of the primary resources that a gardener consumes in the process of making a garden, a fact that doesn't immediately square with notions of resilience. It's also one of the scarcest resources and one you should be mindful of using in support of novel ecosystems. Even if you plant before a rainstorm, you will likely need to supplement nature's precipitation with temporary irrigation as you establish new plantings. Consider how the garden, a novel ecosystem, can produce resources to offset those consumed during its inception.

Beyond any water you may apply to your garden, the flow of natural precipitation confounds as much as it clarifies. Following the line of water, its flow at the surface can yield tremendous insights into how, when, and where to intervene as a gardener. If you live in an upland setting, your landscape has a larger unsaturated zone that can absorb more precipitation, reducing stream recharge and thus lowering flood risks downhill. If you live and garden on a slope, you already understand how essential it is to plant diversely to stabilize the soil and minimize erosion.

Surface water movement makes headline news during flash floods. However, the flow of water beneath the surface is just as important for its long-lasting implications on ecosystem function. Groundwater moves at highly variable speeds in different environments around the world. In some watersheds, groundwater may move from recharge areas to discharge zones at speeds of feet per decade. Research in Iowa prairie restorations and reconstructions illustrates that as deep-rooted grasses and forbs establish and mature, the water table stabilizes at a greater depth. Vegetation bridges life above and belowground.

While a gardener probably doesn't think much about groundwater, the larger and lusher your garden plantings, the more they can impact local water tables. A diverse plant community also impacts how much water runs off versus how much can slowly percolate as different growth habits and root structures create fine-scale networks for water to move through the soil column. In your region, look at how native plant communities stabilize their environments and form a living weft. A thriving mix of stiff and soft-stemmed species, emergent and branching, graminoids, and vines slow water movement on the soil surface and encourage infiltration.

Sedges and rushes deserve special mention. These grass-like plants are invaluable on slopes, drainage ways, and rain gardens, where they mitigate the risks of early-season flooding and erosion caused by snowmelt and spring precipitation. Vernal biological activity delivers ecosystem services. Often, these cool-season and ephemeral species aren't the first

This meadow vignette conveys the availability of its most important resource—water—with bold textures and lushness. Planting design by Bryan Fischer, Gardens on Spring Creek (Fort Collins, Colorado, US).

plants we gravitate towards when designing gardens, but they contribute enormously to fortifying the soil. It's beneficial to plant species in your natural garden that reach peak growth at different times throughout the growing season. This will help protect the soil and promote water filtration all year.

Slopes require strategic planting plans to keep soil in place. Planting design by Kelly Norris, Blank Performing Arts Center (Indianola, Iowa, US).

Nutrients

Food gardeners understand the importance of preserving nutrients in order to maintain productivity, yields, and the sustainability of the harvest. In contrast, dense plant communities are more diverse and complex than agronomic systems or home-scale food gardens. This diversity and complexity create positive feedback loops between plants and soil that, by definition, preserve nutrients within the ecosystem. If you want to integrate home food production activities into the context of your natural garden, you can devise a holistic approach that leverages enhanced soil health with sustainable yields. You can improve the integrity of the soil and reduce nutrient loss to runoff and erosion by reducing tillage, preserving organic matter that accumulates, and integrating trees to capture deep soil nutrients when possible.

Various reports have shown that growing plants for consumption in ecological environments tends to increase yields, though to what effect depends on what you're growing and how you're harvesting it. Increasing plant diversity leads to more complex microbial networks that improve water-holding capacity and nutrient uptake, resulting in increased plant productivity for harvest. Further, any amount of complex vegetation that covers the ground positively impacts soil carbon and greenhouse gas retention versus the alternative. Growing perennial food crops stabilizes soil and nutrient flow disrupted by annual food crop production. This not only mitigates the challenges posed by monoculture systems but also introduces a sustainable model for food production that aligns with ecological principles.

Reduce, Reuse, Recycle

The three R's of late twentieth-century environmentalism often succeed in getting affirmative nods but only modest shifts in behavior. Doing any of those things, though, comes with emotional benefits, sparing some people the guilt of knowing that something would otherwise be wasted. The flip side is that humans readily consume more when they know recycling is an option. Consumption is hard to overcome. As you go about your natural gardening, invest and reinvest resources for the greatest ecological return. Consider these actions:

- **Spend money on more vegetation.** Yes, go buy more plants, particularly those produced locally and in sturdy plastic pots (compared to those flimsy, blow-molded containers that crumple as you untangle the roots). Commercial horticulture is increasingly shifting towards innovative uses of bioplastic, plantable, and compostable containers that use organic or recycled, post-consumer materials, offering a hopeful future for reducing the carbon footprint of planting. Patronizing these options as they become available incentivizes producers to keep offering them, even if they cost slightly more than the alternative.

- **Plant bareroot.** Niche sectors for some trees, shrubs, and perennials continue to sell plants bareroot, which comes with the benefit of a smaller carbon footprint (i.e., often shipped in bulk and without individual plastic pots means less weight). Bareroot plants often establish healthier root systems with a greater likelihood of establishment than larger containerized plants.

- **Don't throw plastic pots away so long as they remain stable.** Reuse these pots for at-home propagation and garden waste after you've given them a quick scrub and rinse to remove any residue that could harbor disease or foster pests. Or look for a local nursery or greenhouse that can repurpose or properly recycle them. More growers and industry partners are offering these solutions as an added value for environmentally conscious consumers.

Repurposing old concrete is a carbon-savvy approach to hardscaping.

- **Repurpose old concrete as hardscaping.** Worldwide, concrete production accounts for almost 9 percent of all human carbon dioxide emissions. Concrete has been used as a building material for thousands of years, and old cities and neighborhoods often have ample refuse. Older concrete often contains a higher mineral aggregate content, lacks rebar or wire reinforcement, and breaks with ease compared to modern products. In the landscape, it takes on an almost stone-like appearance. Washed free of fines, the waste pieces can find new life in gravel gardens as mulch or media for growing stress-tolerant plants.

- **Express yourself with found objects.** Forget new garden tchotchkes. Writers Rob Walker and Joshua Glenn, in their book *Significant Objects*, hypothesized that stories could increase the emotional value of insignificant trinkets, transforming them from the flotsam of consumerism into significant objects. Especially in older neighborhoods or properties, historical ephemera rise to the surface as landscaping alters soil and vegetation. Celebrate these artifacts, patinaed by time, with pride of place, and weave your own narrative of how they came to be. The landscapes we tend to are palimpsests, shaped by time and nature into what we experience today.

Acts of Weeding

Weeding is an unavoidable activity for any gardener, which seeks to resolve what belongs and what doesn't. As a chore, weeding sounds arduous and daunting. Most of us have faced the facts on a weekend afternoon with a sinking feeling in our stomach and a small voice asking, "How did it get this bad?" Perhaps there's more to weeding than the physical, brute task of removing unwanted vegetation. The first question to consider is how those weeds got there in the first place. In natural gardening, you will likely identify weeds as species you've planted and those you haven't. Weeding then becomes an organizing task, one done judiciously.

What Is a Weed?

Weeds have no botanical definition even though in pop culture gardeners like to distinguish them from more desirable, if not generic, "plants." Memes abound—is this a weed or a plant? A weed would seem to be any plant out of place that challenges a gardener's notion of control. But weeds also represent our ignorance. Why should we assume that something spontaneous is unwelcome?

Even if we can't always agree on what is or isn't a weed, most weeds have something in common: they are worthy rivals thriving amid disturbance. In his book *Wild About Weeds*, author Jack Wallington calls weeds "rebel plants," a label that likely stirs strong emotions for some readers. Whether perennial or annual, most plants we frequently judge out of place are what an ecologist would call a ruderal, an opportunist optimized to complete its life cycle amid environmental disturbance. Ruderality is generally a short-lived phenomenon. However, some weeds have also evolved as competitors, dominating site conditions with sheer physical presence, a knack for co-opting resources, or manipulating their immediate microenvironment with root exudates. Even still, some weeds have picked up the ability to persist through withering stresses, such as extended droughts, with deep penetrating taproots or substantial crowns capable of fomenting endless rebellion. Weeds come with a well-stocked arsenal.

Knowing something about the opponent can shed insights into their arrival in a garden environment. As discussed in Section 1: Place, plants reflect features of their environment. Weeds growing in our garden are clues to the nature of place, shedding insights on a legacy of previous activities and reflecting how we go about gardening. Suddenly, ordinary horticultural acts like hoeing, fertilizing, and composting stand in new light. We do these things to create favorable environments for plants we wish to grow. Plants we don't want to grow simply take advantage of the resources. You can beat weeds at their own game if you know how to play. Manipulating the environment to favor what you've planted arguably should happen *before* you commence a new planting, but this isn't always practicable, realistic, or even appropriate for every place.

Eryngium leavenworthii *(Leavenworth's eryngo)*
festoons barbed wire fences and abandoned
paddocks throughout the south-central United
States. Beyond its feral origins, it enjoys a
reputation as a spellbinding annual wildflower.

Sometimes you plant your own weeds like Packera aurea *(golden ragwort). The difference between useful and unfavorable is measured by tolerance.*

What to Weed

Despite our best intentions, the nature of place often comes into sharp focus after the disturbance of planting. Cue weeds unearthed from the seed bank, a reminder that the early years following planting are defined by those species that establish and colonize first (and, of course, you'd rather the "colonists" only be the species you planted). If this cohort includes weeds from the seed bank, you can and should expect their influence on the rest of the plant community. Distinguishing between control and eradication is essential; while control is feasible early, eradication often requires significant resources and may be impractical once weeds are established. Context matters, too; a plant considered a nuisance in one region may serve a vital ecological role elsewhere.

While the first few years are critical for establishing the desired plant community, remember you're playing a long game. If you have limited time, focus on weeds that pose the most significant long-term challenge to favorable species. With perennial weed species, intervention is crucial, as controlling these weeds becomes more challenging as they become established. Annual weeds can inundate and overwhelm plantings, but the goal for controlling them is relatively simple: prevent them from completing their life cycle. While many annual weeds will fade over time, this isn't a reason to ignore them, as some species with robust growth can overcome planted species with conservative habits that may take a few years to settle in. Even if you can't pull every plant, removing seeds before they ripen can break the cycle with the least disturbance. While there are few prizes for diligent weeding in a natural garden, there is an honorable mention for being thorough and consistent in the early life of a new planting. This work pays dividends.

Until now, most of this essay reads with the usual tone of a gardener discussing weeding: overtures to military conflict, strategies, and tactics. Battle, enemy, arsenal, and a hundred other related words have strangely entered the horticultural lexicon to describe engagement with those species we don't want in our gardens.

Encouraging the spontaneity of a species like Erigeron annuus *(annual fleabane) comes with the responsibility to ensure they don't overstay their welcome.*

Yet, the nature of our interactions with plants and landscapes shouldn't be militant. We can adjudicate and negotiate a mutual coexistence by understanding how plants arrived and how they might leave. Even the most pernicious threats to biodiversity in various parts of the world—purple loosestrife in the United States or Canada goldenrod in Europe—remain well established beyond our wit's end. Engaging with these species is, at best, a subject of control; a mountain of data from so-called "invasion biology" suggests that eradication at landscape scale is ineffective and implausible. This isn't the white flag of surrender because nobody should be at war with plants. Many of these weeds, especially non-native ones, are abundant because of human activities.

In the garden, one of the primary life-giving forces to undesirable plants is organic pollution, the over-enrichment of soils as a legacy of previous gardening or agriculture. While mitigating this after the fact requires time, if you garden in highly fertile soil, minimize the amount of organic material that returns annually. You may haul this away for composting rather than leaving it as a duff on the soil's surface. Regardless, there will always be weeds because something will always be out of place. The medium of a garden provides the space for asking and answering such questions. Every plant can't grow everywhere.

Deadheading

Deadheading is one of those activities that some gardeners have more of a preference for than others. I find it fussy; others find it fulfilling—yes, of course, some things look utterly bedraggled if left to hang in repose atop tall stems. Many species with indeterminate growth habits will keep giving, producing an unstoppable parade of flowers that keeps pollinators fulfilled. Suspending deadheading a month before the first frost ensures that plants begin to transition from active growth into dormancy, with maybe a few seeds along the way.

Beyond aesthetic tolerances, deadheading is a valid tool for an ecological gardener if you're doing it to consciously keep seedy things at bay, your snippety hands mimicking some browsing animal or bird. This rectifying disturbance invokes some balance and order in the composition of the plant community. Conversely, take the activity so far as botanical beheading, and you could easily rob the planting of the very force that gives it natural weft and entropy. Even the flowers you miss may have value for wildlife in seed, which may further reduce their spread the following season depending on what creatures consume the fruits.

The Art of Removal

Weeding simulates grazing, a natural activity that would lop off biomass at multiple points in the growing year. How you weed is as important as what you weed. The method depends on the species in your sights and the context of where you're working.

For most perennial weeds, liberate the root system from the ground, so long as you don't disturb too much soil. If you disturb too much soil, your weeding efforts may be counterproductive. If that's the case, take a frugal approach and rob it of the resources to thrive and reproduce. I remember experimenting in a corner of the garden with three or four different commercially made "dandelion diggers" some years ago. The garden looked worse for the effort, almost as if a feral pig had rooted around for a meal. What I failed to do at that moment was lean into the disturbance and plant something. Doing so might have clarified the exercise from one of intervention to one of rejuvenation. In the end, other weed species germinated and took their place, although eventually were crowded out by a thriving stand of *Tridens flavus* (purpletop) in the years to come. In this tiny microcosm of our front yard, three episodes played out, each with different characters and outcomes in a few years. In this instance, hindsight offered tremendous clarity on the intensity of my actions.

In mineral-based soils, sweep with a hoe as space between plants permits, leveraging the texture of the soil to your advantage and scaling the surface area for wholesale efficiency. While you may bring seeds to the surface, you may also cultivate a new generation of species you want, cast off as a new generation from last year's flowering. As gaps close, you can refine your approach to the circumstances of your planting, increasing the precision or the length of time between weedings. Between rocks and hard places, strive for

In our meadow, we've encouraged the weedy Tridens flavus *(purpletop), replacing one weed for another but with more ecological value to the garden.*

thoroughness because any decaying organic matter only spawns another generation of plants otherwise well-adapted to the stress of the crevice. The action is based on the environmental circumstance and the plants you seek to manage.

In the meadow, pull weeds diligently in the early seasons of establishment and consider mechanical interventions carefully. A grassland plant community exists because of the rich life thriving in the thatchy crust of organic matter below the crowns of plants and into the first few inches (7 to 10 cm) of soil. As grasses and forbs form this weft over time, try not to disturb their root zones more than necessary. Remember that weeds of older, established meadow plantings tend to tolerate the routine stress of grazing (mowing) by keeping adventitious shoots proximal to their crowns. Cutting them off at or near the surface reduces the likelihood of regeneration.

Learning to leave the remnants of last season challenges cultural notions of tidiness. But how can you deny this Panicum virgatum *(switchgrass) the chance to shine through to the end of winter?*

Again

Tidiness pervades garden culture, a strange domain for human behavior that seems tenuously in place elsewhere. Evolutionary scholars suggest that tidiness is an antidote to disgust, an emotional response triggered by the senses and memories of situations that revulse or scare us. This emotion is irrational, which manifests in contradictory behaviors like frequently mowing lawns while neglecting laundry or handwashing.

In the garden, we have strange proxies for order. Grass left long, where kids otherwise run and play, inspires fears of ticks, mites, and snakes while also suggesting a lack of care. An abundance of green growth with little color can stimulate feelings of neglect or trigger a concern that plant growth has surpassed a gardener's abilities. While you may find these cultural norms annoying and dated, your partner, family, or neighbors might not.

More recently, the globally popular No Mow May campaign has instigated a cross-examination of tidiness and naturalness from the lawn to the perennial border. No Mow May originated with the UK-based conservation organization Plantlife and has gained a foothold in other parts of the world. When gardeners sprint at the first warm weather to cut back the garden—an act enshrined in the vocabulary as "spring cleanup"—advocates of the alternative insist on waiting.

The logic has merits. Leaving the lawn unmown or last year's vegetation standing for just a few more weeks provides an extended period for overwintering invertebrates to reawaken from diapause and begin their life cycles, not to mention promoting early floral resources that might succumb to the "cleanup." In the United Kingdom, unlike the United States, there is less obsession with turfgrass monocultures and a more diverse island flora, making it more likely for flowery lawns to replace well-shorn greens. Dark European honeybees (*Apis mellifera mellifera*) also call the island home, having evolved with dandelions and many of northern Europe's beloved wildflowers (which, when transported to the United States, are then called "weeds"). In the United States, where green monocultures supported by fertilizers and herbicides have reigned culturally supreme for decades, the average unmown lawn at best supports a mix of turfgrasses and whatever ruderal species have adapted to the disturbance regime for biweekly mowing (read: dandelions, white clover, and perhaps a few native violets). In the border or hedgerow, you could make a stronger case that delaying intervention permits more life to flourish. But how long do you hold off before new growth complicates the chore?

The precision of timing depends on the circumstances. In the mosaic of a natural landscape, every plot of earth experiences the beginning and conclusion of the season differently from year to year. In some natural systems, late-season fires wipe the slate clean long before winter sets in, rejuvenating some species to return the following spring with verve. In other places, biomass steadily accumulates, feeding a hungry force of decomposers that convert organic matter from one form into another. The natural gardener's challenge is two-fold: how to "do no harm" in a landscape that serves some horticultural, aesthetic purpose.

Spring is not a time for cleaning but a season for resetting. Respecting the complexity of life should inspire reflection on how to proceed with what's often a set of prescribed horticultural tasks. Traditionally, "cleaning up" the garden is an act of liberation, clearing the runway for prized specimens to lead an unhindered life. In ecological terms, restarting the garden is an intervention of low intensity, allowing plants and the life they support to proceed unheeded. While raking, gathering, and mowing might top the chore list in spring, different plant communities vary in requirements. Ascertain accordingly, but don't be shy about erring with confidence in plant resilience. Nobody rakes the woodland floor or picks up sticks along the floodplain, just as no blade runs across the prairie or grassland. Flora and fauna thrive in these places. What you have to decide is how to promote life and preserve legibility.

First, watch and observe. Much gets made of oversimplified suggestions like waiting until the temperature exceeds a certain threshold for a specific number of days. It's well-intended advice and perhaps a generic barometer, but animals of all stripes don't always follow suit. As best we know, insects emerge from diapause due to temperature and photoperiod, but the specific mechanisms vary between and even within species. Your knowledge and observations of seasonal conditions can help inform your timing. If you notice signs of life after winter, don't let eagerness govern your schedule. Delaying disturbance by even a week or two increases the likelihood that more overwintering organisms have had a chance to commence with their new year. Plants with indeterminate growth habits will recover in earnest even if they encounter any vernal impediments like last year's debris.

The timing for starting the garden again varies widely with weather and geography. Watch the landscape for cues and be conscious of how much disturbance you introduce.

Second, don't do the same thing simultaneously for over two years. Consider a rotational strategy for which parts of the garden you cut back or restart first. By creating a mosaic of conditions, you can ensure that the same portion of habitat isn't affected by otherwise routine interventions. Unpredictable spring weather in some parts of the world almost assuredly results in such chronological variation anyway.

Regardless of exactly when you strike out to cut back the garden, do you ever wonder why we've made such a big fuss about "cleaning" it up in the first place? Are the remnants of the last growing season dirty? As naturally inspired gardening encourages more people to consider putting plants in the lead, some aesthetic norms might soften or shift altogether. We can hope. In the meantime, every gardener has to wrestle with notions of care nested within the garden's annual life cycle. Would you rather be tidy or timely?

Into the Woods

Both deciduous and coniferous forests and woodlands cover substantial acres of the Earth's surface. As humans have developed cities, we've planted trees for shade and as tokens of environmental stewardship. Thus, for many gardeners, forest ecology looms over the fundamentals of home gardening. Defining tree-dominated ecosystems becomes a parlor game—how much canopy matters? Generally speaking, a forest covers more than 75 percent of the ground with tree canopy, as compared to a woodland, which has 30 to 50 percent, and a savanna or scrubland, which has 10 to 30 percent canopy.

The nature of the openings sometimes matters more than the total canopy coverage, especially from the perspective of the gardener puttering around at ground level. While gaps obviously arise from falling trees, the construction of homes or other structures creates openings in the canopy for your gardening activities that ripple outward. From the ecosystem perspective, this sudden influx of sunlight creates a microhabitat that is warmer and more exposed than the surrounding forest, making it an ideal environment for the growth of shade-intolerant and edge species, contributing to a burst of productivity and biodiversity. Over time, these gaps contribute significantly to the structural heterogeneity and species diversity of forests. They provide opportunities for a variety of species to coexist by creating a mosaic of habitats with different light and moisture conditions. More gardening may happen in the cool shade of our neighboring trees, a place of shelter and contemplation for looking out into an increasingly warming world.

Site Conditions

Forest plant communities often feature diverse layers formed by diverse tree species, including generally closed and well-developed canopies with middle canopy and understory layers below. If you live and garden in a forested region in the developed world, you undoubtedly do so under the canopy of second-growth forests, now a generation removed from so-called "intact forests" that existed prior to human settlement or modern industry. Excluding human disturbance, a primary driver of soil composition in forests in the northern hemisphere is the extent to which they've been glaciated. Unglaciated soils are geologically older and generally somewhat more acidic but can span the gamut from sand to clay in texture. Depending on the nature of the soil and its topography, forest soils can easily erode, especially if subsoil compaction occurs during disturbance events like logging or home construction. The accumulation of litter in the understory prevents erosion and helps the soil retain water.

When gardening and managing vegetation in forested environments, you need to consider the cycle of water throughout the year. By virtue of vertically layered vegetation, forests are uniquely structured environments that capture precipitation at many levels. The upper canopy absorbs most of the volume of rainfall, some of which evaporates back into the atmosphere while a smaller portion finds its way to the ground. The result is an often humid understory as water vapor gets trapped closer to the surface, though this depends to a large part on the presence of shrubs and density of herbaceous vegetation. In some parts of the world, forests receive even moisture across the calendar, whereas other regions experience seasonal extremes with abundant precipitation in one or a few seasons.

Peering into a bright opening from the green shelter of the Asian Woods, Chanticleer (Wayne, Pennsylvania, US). In a warming world, the future of many home gardens is undoubtedly under canopy.

In this floodplain forest, Chasmanthium latifolium *(northern river oats) blankets the understory in a vast matrix interrupted by a young canopy of* Acer saccharinum *(silver maple) and* A. negundo *(box elder).*

In more open woodland environments, greater complexity of understory and middle canopy species can often lead to increased water consumption, resulting in a drier environment by mid-growing season. Under natural circumstances, a fire would have naturally disturbed these ecosystems, drawing down organic matter and stimulating the populations of species under competition from larger, leafier plants. Drought also affects these ecosystems, with more plants vying for less and less water. Understanding these moisture dynamics helps to contextualize your gardening efforts—the conditions affect how many and what kinds of species can grow in a stressful environment.

Planting

As you undertake planting interventions in forest ecosystems, evaluate the existing condition to determine the extent of your efforts. If your site is home to many non-native species that have colonized in the wake of disturbance, you will need to remove or control them for the effective establishment of the designed plant community. You may also find that your place is already home to desirable plants if only you knew their name. Abundant resources, including many apps powered by artificial intelligence, exist for chipping away at the great biological unknowns of your backyard. If you can name it, you can understand it. Preserving existing vegetation in the woodland understory only slightly complicates site preparation and planting (i.e., How do you preserve some plants and kill others without annihilating everything by accident?).

You should also evaluate the litter accumulation in the understory and decide whether removing some of that biomass will ease the planting and establishment process. In areas with higher wildfire frequencies, you may do this simply to reduce the fuel load. In the end, the cycle of that biomass is a feature of the system, not a bug to be fixed. Consider how your gardening runs alongside the accumulation and decomposition of organic matter and how you can supplement or leaven the process.

Woodland environments offer another surface for sensory exploration—bark. The ridge and valley pattern of Populus grandidentata *(bigtooth aspen) bark also doubles as a habitat for insects and a feeding ground for birds and mammals.*

In general, avoid drastic disturbances to the surface roots of desirable species that could otherwise negatively impact the existing canopy. If you're interested in diversifying the age structure of the canopy under which you garden, consider establishing trees as small saplings or directly from seed. This kind of effort requires thoughtful planning so that the evolution of a new canopy layer doesn't conflict with the user experience of the garden or reduce short-term niche diversity for other species, particularly on small properties or projects. You may even consider raising small nursery stands of trees and eventually selecting one or a few dominant specimens to continue their development into canopy specimens.

Many woodland understory species, particularly those native to the Northern Hemisphere with ephemeral life histories, establish readily en masse as bare-root plants. Reputable nurseries raise these in production beds from seed or division, multiplying them under ideal conditions for easy lifting and harvesting. These are often best planted in the cool seasons of the year and may not readily form visible populations for the first few seasons until well-established in their new home. If your site is in a seminatural condition, watch for native species that may already be present. Your initial planting efforts should bolster those existing populations in service to your long-term goals.

If you endeavor to create a forest ecosystem from a presently open environment, you'll want to consider the succession of pioneer species to mature canopy species. This process will unfold as a beautiful thicket over many decades, relying heavily on natural succession as the key driver of spatial complexity. Early successional species live fast and die young, providing an initial amount of shade that fosters microenvironments for seedling canopy species to establish. You may undertake this project in phases, planting out several layers of the forest over many years, or as a cohort, establishing both early and late successional species initially and monitoring the community development over time. Research has shown that some species, like *Liriodendron tulipifera* (tulip poplar), can accelerate the development of forest ecosystems due to their fast growth and canopy development. In general, as shade increases and microclimates develop, the overall character of a forest comes into focus. Bluntly speaking, this process isn't for the impatient.

The Miyawaki method, developed by Japanese botanist Akira Miyawaki, is a way to establish dense, fast-growing forests. The Miyawaki Method involves several key steps: First, the soil is worked on to enhance its oxygenation and enrichment with organic matter. This process, which can take anywhere from three days to two weeks, involves loosening the soil, incorporating organic matter, and covering it with mulch. Next, species native to the local ecosystem are selected and planted at a high density. This not only ensures a diverse mix of plant life but also encourages healthy competition among the plants, which can lead to accelerated growth. Finally, the new forest is covered with mulch, which helps to conserve moisture and suppress weeds. During establishment, the developing forest uses less water than sparser tree plantings and generally requires little intervention unless trees pose a threat to human safety.

Scutellaria incana *(hoary skullcap), a North American native of open woodland edges.*

Management and Stewardship

In residential settings within forested environments, managing the integrity of the canopy is your primary objective. As canopies become more closed, niche diversity decreases. Conversely, as canopies open, the supply of organic matter that accumulates from leaf fall decreases. While this can be counteracted by understory vegetation to some extent, the loss of canopy sets in motion the progression from one state of forest to another. Maximize light whenever possible while preserving the canopy coverage necessary for the environment to still be a forest. Your actions on a small plot may involve removing smaller saplings to create a competitive bias for those with more robust habits. Research shows that in many woodland environments, selective removals can increase the rate of productivity in the overall system. You can apply this same management strategy to hedgerows or windbreaks as you work to increase their complexity while hastening their maturation.

In your gardening, you may strike a balance between how much organic matter accumulates and what time frame you allow for its decomposition. Coniferous trees generally have lower nutrient requirements than deciduous species. Many conifers can thrive on rocky, lean, nutrient-poor soils, in part because of how their needles have evolved to capture water and reduce transpiration. Understory litter below coniferous species accumulates and breaks down more slowly at the surface than under deciduous canopies. In forests with substantial deciduous canopies, the understory remains generally moist throughout the year, in part thanks to the buildup of organic matter. Under any canopy, ground-level organic matter becomes an organizing element of the understory. Decomposition always increases towards the edge with the most sunlight.

Cities across the world support hybrid mixtures of native and non-native woody species that often form novel urban forests. Trees in these environments frequently attempt to colonize horticultural environments from which they may have even originated. Knowing the composition of nearby forest plots helps you predict potential weed pressures or identify adventive newcomers (depending on both your perspective and the species in question).

Weed management in woodland settings thus applies to both canopy and understory species. For undesirable woody species, hand pulling is easiest at the residential scale so long as you can both surveil and identify them while they're young. If allowed to develop wood and increase in girth, girdling may work for some species but is not universally effective. A significant arsenal of herbicides exists for managing woody vegetation, but can have mixed results depending on its intended target and application. Further, using herbicides around established, designed plant communities often presents more headaches than solutions. Prevention is always advisable but rests heavily on surveillance and early detection. Understory weed species play a stiff hand; they've evolved the same mechanism for surviving as desirable vegetation has, withstanding low light and sometimes limited water resources. Some problematic species, like *Microstegium vimineum* (Japanese stiltgrass), may prove impossible to eradicate, leaving control as a more pragmatic option. While stiltgrass responds to low-intensity understory fires, burning is not likely available to homeowners as a safe and effective control method. Many understory weed species will require a combination of control methods such as mowing, tilling, and herbicide in tandem to reduce their populations below viable thresholds. In general, control is only effective when populations cease to reproduce or recruit new individuals from the seed bank. For species that spread vegetatively, this can prove especially difficult.

Quilted matrices make for texturally rich understory plantings as light availability increases. Planting design by Nigel Dunnett, Barbican Centre (London, UK).

Absent fire, you have to consider how your gardening activities can reduce the biomass of some species when necessary. You may do this for both aesthetic and ecological reasons. While many forest or woodland garden plantings flourish after initial establishment, changes in the canopy composition will warrant the addition of plants and populations over time unless you choose to rely on natural succession and seedling recruitment alone. In an urban environment, this method won't always produce results sufficient for the timescale of residential gardening.

Early summer in our front yard Meadow Nord at Three Oaks Garden (Des Moines, Iowa, US).

Meadows and Prairies

Meadows enjoy increasing popularity as more gardeners embrace natural possibilities within otherwise horticultural environments. A meadow is a place of consilience, an intervention with wildness that's both intentional and humble. It's perhaps the most primitive kind of garden in human history, a clearing in the woods or a disturbance within a vaster plain. Even our lawns are meadows, though often reduced to the smallest denominator of a few readily mown species. As you live with a designed grassland or meadow plant community, your primary goal is to preserve its openness. In some parts of the world, this chore is daunting against the steady advance of climate-adapted woody plants with surging canopies. But as you toil, succumb to the romance of grasslands, an almost musical experience replete with lyrics, percussion, and harmony. In many places, a meadow home garden sounds just right.

Site Conditions

Understanding initial site conditions is key to creating high-quality, grassland-inspired plantings. Grassland vegetation can develop on almost any range of soil moisture regimes—xeric to hydric—and across a range of seasonal precipitation patterns. As you look towards natural references or adapt them for use in the home garden, consider the composition and structure of the desired vegetation by understanding how they formed under annual precipitation patterns and atop underlying topography. Whatever inspiration you derive has roots and stems in the context of place.

The cycle between wet and dry periods in a growing year indicates what kind of vegetation thrives in a particular season. A wet prairie, for instance, generally grows under inundation for some period of the growing season but may experience wide variation in moisture availability in a single year (e.g., flood springs and droughty summers). Tall, emergent, late-flowering perennials dominate wet prairies after imbibing spring precipitation to leap to towering heights. Contrast that with a mid-elevation karst meadow with alkaline-adapted plant species. While this community may occur in regions with abundant rainfall, rocky soils drain quickly or irregularly, leading to an overall dry but patchy moisture regime. Species grow accordingly, achieving similar sizes across the community due to fixed available resources.

In grassland systems, even slight changes in topography at the surface of the soil can lead to microclimates that support different species composition. Microtopography can inform how and when snow melts in spring, which plants are exposed to desiccating winds, and where organic matter accumulates at the end of the growing year. Existing plantings often contain these signatures. Grasslands are often mosaics of plant communities reflecting underlying site conditions, even when they appear visually consistent.

*This meadow utilizes a single grass species—*Sporobolus heterolepis *(prairie dropseed)—to create a unified matrix, which makes for easier weed surveillance. Planting design by Roy Diblik and Jeff Epping, Olbrich Botanical Gardens (Madison, Wisconsin, US).*

Planting

Preparing a site for meadow-like vegetation requires careful analysis of the existing soil condition. Site preparation can be resource intensive, front-loading costs that the landscape pays back in time with appreciable gains in vegetation density. Regardless of the method or the setting, you want to reduce or eliminate competition from existing weed species, if present. If you're beginning with turfgrass that's been traditionally managed with herbicides and routine mowing, the underlying weed seed bank may be limited. While deep legacies from agriculture and urban development have altered the structural characteristics of soils, planting in this condition may yield positive results quickly due to limited weed competition. In other cases, those past disturbances may have oxidized the soil, which affects the availability of nutrients to plant roots and will slow the establishment of desirable vegetation. In these situations, routine weed surveillance may extend into the third or even fourth season after establishment until the planting canopy closes.

If establishing meadows in dry or degraded environments, you may introduce plant cohorts at different times. If you aim to support various plant species for consistent floral displays, introducing vigorous species early may limit niche opportunities. Instead, consider planting a diverse cohort of forbs in the first year, followed by the addition of grasses in the following year. Conversely, if you need a quicker and cheaper approach, you could plant grasses and vigorous species first to cover the ground quickly and begin soil restoration. Additional planting could occur later as overall conditions improve, although you'll have to reduce or remove the biomass of the founder cohort to make way for new additions.

In general, deep tillage should be avoided when at all possible. Regardless of the underlying soil condition, the benefits of additional aeration from deep tillage are almost always negated by the destruction of soil microorganisms and their networks. In compacted soils, short-term gains in aeration may quickly give way to even more severe compaction once the soil reaggregates. Cover crops are a viable and attractive option for many sites, particularly if you can wait for a season for these often fast-growing annual species to do their work. Trusting plant roots to do the work is the hardest and yet wisest thing a naturally inclined gardener can do. The results may take time but are worth the wait.

Most restoration manuals and handbooks prescribe a regime of surface tillage and herbicide application, which have scalable results on large projects. Surface disking or cultipacking the top few inches (7 to 10 cm) has benefits when immediately followed by seeding or planting. In the residential setting, one or two applications of broad-spectrum herbicides like glyphosate can be effective if the existing vegetation is too dense to foster the development of a desirable plant community. Organic approaches are also effective within appropriate time frames (i.e., several weeks or months depending on practice). It's important to remember that there is no morally righteous way to establish a planting; either scenario results in the disruption or death of soil-borne organisms.

The timing of establishment will depend on your climate, goals, and desired plant communities. While prescriptions abound for specific regions, consider a few basic ideas:

- Fall sowings and plantings benefit from cooler temperatures and precipitation patterns; you'll often irrigate these less and experience a shorter period of establishment before winter sets in. If sowing from seed, this timing will favor those species that need a cold period to germinate (stratification). Most research in prairie establishment suggests that fall planting favors forb establishment over the long term.

In this residential dry meadow, a shortgrass matrix of Bouteloua gracilis *'Honeycomb' (Honeycomb blue grama grass) is interrupted by silvery fumes of* Andropogon gerardii *'Holy Smoke' (Holy Smoke big bluestem). Planting design by Kelly Norris.*

- Spring sowings and plantings benefit from warming soil temperatures, a condition conducive to the germination of warm-season grasses. This timing can often produce rapid results but with different levels of diversity and composition (i.e., more grass-dominant or biased towards less diversity and early successional species). Spring plantings and sowings often require intensive weed management in the first season, given that the disturbance of establishment favors the rapid germination and development of annual species seizing the opportunity to grow. Mid- and late-summer mowings may be required for larger areas.

- New research is beginning to illustrate the significance of a phenomenon called "year effects," which describes the variation in vegetation composition and structure that results when the same method executed in different seasons produces different results. You may find the most value in starting with a few areas of your landscape and slowly expanding with time as you learn more about the place and how plantings respond. Supplemental plantings are not uncommon.

- For prairies and meadows, most practical experience and research conclude that watering deeply and infrequently during the establishment period hastens results. The duration of the establishment period will vary with climate, geography, and timing, from as little as a week to several months of the first growing season. Much like fertilizing, in general, broad-spectrum irrigation encourages weed pressures.

Management and Stewardship

Ideally, before you commence a planting inspired by grassland vegetation, you should consider how your management activities will mimic natural disturbances, including the lives of large animals that once called them home. Disturbances in grassland systems encourage niche diversity by tilting, if only briefly, the scale of competition away from vigorous, dominant species (usually grasses).

The size of your landscape and its surroundings will inform what practices make sense. Can you burn it? If not, is mowing your only option? Historic fire patterns preserved a certain level of species diversity over time that may not be easily replicated in a residential setting without fire. In small spaces, hand weeding at regular intervals in the first few seasons after planting might serve your purposes. But as the area of a planting increases, you will need to consider more mechanical or easily scaled options. Weed management in the first year or two after planting is critical, especially when weed species compete for similar

niches as desired species. Dense weed canopies in the early years of a new planting can shade out and rob desirable vegetation of water, particularly so when established from seed. Annual weed species are rarely problematic long term, but perennial species can prove pernicious if they establish early and alongside your intended plant community.

Over many years, promoting a florally rich meadow requires a delicate balance of interventions. In recent natural history, meadows and prairies flourished after some initial disturbance—fire, grazing, haying—reduced the volume of grassy species and released forbs from their competitive pressure. As this tango between life forms continues, grasses rush the line, occupying more niches by converting soil nutrients into biomass. As they grow larger, forbs lose ground until the next disturbance event repeats the cycle. In another rendition of this cadence, some perennial forbs can gain equal footing with grasses. In the United Kingdom and northern Europe, historic agricultural rotations of grazing and haying reduced grass abundance in favor of cool-season flowering plants. Variations in this method across the greater landscape produced a rich mosaic of habitats for a great abundance of plants and animals.

Translating this into horticultural practice requires nuance and modification. First, consider the plant community's composition relative to your environment. In parts of the world with ample cool-season plant palettes, including C3 grasses, you may cut the vegetation between cool periods (i.e., mid to late summer) and when the stress of warm weather results in quasi-dormancy (though watch for weeds that might take advantage of this window of opportunity). In warm-season grassland systems, the routine flips to the shoulders of the growing season, with the clearance of growth happening in fall or late winter and with respective trade-offs for cool-season weeds. Fall grazing or burning, as would be appropriate in warm-season dominated plantings, reduces short-term habitat availability for invertebrates, small

A dramatic collision of south-central US natives evokes a roadside prairie community: Yucca flaccida *(weak-leaf yucca),* Amsonia hubrichtii *(threadleaf bluestar), and* Eragrostis spectabilis *(purple lovegrass).*

mammals, and birds but stimulates forb abundance in the following season. Late winter or early spring cutbacks can release cool-season species to thrive with newfound light but can also favor warm-season grasses as they release from dormancy. Even in these warm-season plantings, you can simulate grazing with midsummer mowing or cutting, which also helps with weed control. However, most gardeners blanch at the idea of swinging a scythe on the eve of summer in hopes of a hefty return in fall or the following spring. It seems *too* disruptive and not culturally appropriate for a space construed as an extension of human habitat. But as some grass species flourish, you could mow the crowns of only those species without your neighbors thinking you've lost your mind. They tend to rebound quickly but, in doing so, draw down reserves that could otherwise have supported unchecked growth.

In general, mowing produces significant biomass. For late-winter and early-spring cutting, this material may be left in place as a mulch or removed entirely depending on the species composition of the planting. In many garden settings, leaving the organic matter to decompose slowly and form a weed-preventing duff has considerable benefits in the years immediately following establishment. As plantings mature, some mown biomass might prove too heavy and require removal so as not to impede growth. This site-specific intuition develops with time and experience. The proliferation of grass species is one of the long-term effects of annual or seasonal mowing in horticultural plantings. Absent fire, these grazing-adapted species flourish under this repetitive management strategy. This may lead to additional planting, replanting, or modulation of activities to compensate for or counteract their success.

Mowing and mulching with duff usually have a short-term negative impact on insect populations. The timing of mowing treads a fine line between preserving insect biodiversity and the ecological integrity of plantings. Research conducted in meadow clearings of German forests showed varying effects on invertebrate groups depending on the timing of mowing. The results, perhaps surprisingly, favored fall mowings as an optimal approach for supporting pollinating insects while reducing disturbance for overwintering insects. Regardless of the exact timing, avoid dogmatic gardening; vary your approach from year to year to spread around the trade-offs between groups of organisms.

At the entrance to the Santa Fe Botanic Garden (Santa Fe, New Mexico, US), a rhythmic vignette of the region's high desert, pinion-juniper woodland vegetation defines a sense of place. Landscape design by W. Gary Smith.

Arid Lands

The complexity of ecology in arid lands makes gardening interventions challenging, if not also deeply rewarding. In these arid landscapes, every drop of water is precious, and the intense sunlight shapes the daily rhythm of both plants and gardeners. Desert plant species are studies in resilience, thriving amid the hardships imposed by limited water, baking temperatures, desiccating wind, and low nutrients. Deserts and arid lands around the world creak under the pressures of human disturbance and absent life-giving resources that fuel rapid recoveries. Human development has encroached most notably on the hydrology of these ecosystems, diverting water to supply cities at the expense of both surface water and underground reserves. These changes echo across the landscape, altering soil chemistry and creating novel environments readily colonized by emergent newcomers. These new species set in motion often irreversible processes, leading deserts into an increasingly hazy future, proverbially and literally, as the changes often increase the ecosystem's susceptibility to wildfires.

Site Conditions

Deserts receive less than 10 inches (25.4 cm) of precipitation per year and can have considerable temperature extremes between day and night. The aridity of deserts is primarily due to their location on the Earth's surface, often in high-pressure zones where dry air descends, or due to the rain shadow effect created by mountain ranges. While aridity defines deserts, temperature regimes define the seasonal environment plants experience. Hot deserts experience warm temperatures during the day followed by cool temperatures at night. Cold deserts experience warm summers but frigid winters, often incurring more winter precipitation than hot deserts. Plant communities native to each of these regions may have common components of the same continental flora but vary greatly in abundance and local specificity based on these conditions. The word *desert* has different meanings depending on the context; not all deserts are the same.

Desert soils trend alkaline in the absence of rain that otherwise would leach away the accumulation of minerals. As a result, desert soils are often shallow and have high salt concentrations. Biological soil crusts, complex communities formed from cyanobacteria and other microbes, are the primary producers of desert ecosystems. They help prevent soil erosion, minimize aridification, and feature prominently in nutrient cycling and nitrogen fixation processes. Preserving microbiotic crusts, when still present, is paramount for the resilience of desert ecosystems; if you have it, don't bust the crust. Restoring biological soil crusts artificially has been largely unsuccessful in landscape-scale experiments, although research continues. However, crusts can recover naturally and recolonize as their components can travel over long and short distances in the air.

Desert soils vary extensively in texture, which can have a dramatic effect on the kind and quality of vegetation that is established. In residential developments, most native soil has been disturbed, compacted, or replaced with imported soil, which can lead to uneven conditions even in relatively similar places. Sandy or coarse textured loams allow for greater water infiltration than sandy clays.

At the landscape scale, desert life thrives from pulses of resources that become available for limited periods of time. Water and nutrient availability varies dramatically across the desert floor, sometimes drastically in the space of a few hundred square feet (28 to 46 m²). Shrubs form an organizing theme of desert plant communities, creating sheltering islands that accumulate nutrients and biodiversity often along arroyos. These gullies fill and flow seasonally after sufficient rain, shaping vegetation patterns that thrive amid intermittent wet conditions.

The presence of native stone in the desert conveys a palpable sense of place and local history, humbling forms along which to inscribe a garden.

Planting

Depending on your initial site conditions, you may already have sufficient protection from winds. If not, you can borrow tools from restoration ecology and consider planting barriers of shrubs or using vertically oriented brush to create windbreaks. Microclimates form inside these spaces, shifting surface water flow and fostering vegetation development. Manipulating the microtopography of the landscape can capture water after monsoon events when they occur and improve permeability. These safe havens foster more consistent seed germination and seedling development. You could adopt the mindset that your whole garden is one of these ecological islands, a place of conscious resource use towards net community vibrancy.

Establishing designed plant communities in the desert requires more than simply arranging plants spatially and aesthetically. The themes of failure are more acute in harsh environments: improper site preparation, poor seeding or planting techniques, improper plant selection based on the resources available, or improper timing. To establish the vegetation effectively, consider the following questions en route to durable assumptions:

Superblooms, like this one captured in Joshua Tree National Park (California, US), occur around the world when optimal temperatures and rainfall spur rapid germination and population development of ruderal species.

Echinocereus engelmannii (strawberry hedgehog cactus) shelters seedlings of annuals like Eschscholzia californica *(California poppy) and* Rafinesquia neomexicana *(desert chicory) from herbivory and erosion.*

- How will you shade young plants, if needed, or protect them for a period of time from intense solar radiation?

- How will you protect the surface of the ground from high temperatures and high winds? What kinds of mulch, if any, will you use to slow the evaporation of water from the soil?

- What is your plan for irrigation or water capture from rainfall events? Have you timed your plantings to take advantage of the greatest chance for natural precipitation? If relying on irrigation water, do you have a consistent supply for the duration of the establishment period?

- How will you mitigate herbivory (if using plants) or granivory (if using seeds)? Young plantings and seedings serve as a buffet to many animals that depend on fresh succulent growth or seeds for survival. You may have just planted the most abundant food supply depending on your local environment. How will you protect the planting to at least foster its establishment so that it may eventually yield more sustainable ecosystem services?

No plant is fully stress-tolerant or resilient unless well-established. Consider establishing plantings from deep plugs and pots with high root-to-shoot ratios for optimal plant survival. Planting projects will require irrigation for a lengthy establishment period. Take care with watering to avoid leaching soils or unnecessary surface runoff. Water slowly and deeply, either by hand or with temporary drip irrigation systems. Seedings offer a more water-sensitive alternative for establishing plantings at larger scales. Even still, seedings may take several years to fully reveal their character. Timing plantings or seedings in the cool seasons increases the likelihood of encountering favorable weather that hastens the success of the project. Using organic mulches appropriately can provide short-term benefits for new plantings, giving them a low dosage of nutrients while promoting deep root growth.

In desert gardening, you may think about developing plantings in phases that mirror natural processes, utilizing some species to foster the establishment of others. If your existing soil condition is highly disturbed, consider establishing woody legumes that naturally form symbiotic associations with rhizobial bacteria and mycorrhizal fungi. Research in desert and dune restorations has shown that using these species as founders leads to improved soil fertility and the successful establishment of other plants as site conditions improve. Further, establishing an "infrastructure" layer can give you early evidence of what types of plants work on the site. You may continue to augment this layer and future layers with additional planting over time until you start to see regeneration or population development. Engaging with a diverse plant palette provides creative tools for adapting to environmental stress.

This xeric planting at Tulsa Botanic Garden (Tulsa, Oklahoma, US) on the doorstep of the western Great Plains marries elements of steppe and desert regions, forecasting a warmer and drier future.

Management and Stewardship

Water conservation is the most fundamental idea for establishing resilient desert vegetation. Even the best water conservation strategies may yield inconsistent plantings, requiring multiple rounds of installation to achieve the desired level of abundance. Managing undesirable vegetation can also have a positive impact on water use.

Nitrogen in soils is generally limited in arid environments. Legacies of past agricultural activities can linger, supporting adventive plant species that wouldn't otherwise survive beyond that altered microenvironment. Previous tillage may have also disturbed natural soil horizons and already shallow water tables, leading to confounded soil structure and drainage issues.

Many of the most pernicious weed species in desert biomes challenge even the most equipped land managers and gardeners. While you may not be content to shrug your shoulders, you should remember the difference between eradication and control. Your gardening over time may work to reduce the biomass of these plants or prohibit their encroachment on more desirable vegetation. Dedicated hand removal is always an option, although with mixed results depending on which species you attempt to control. Some annual weed species may prove beneficial in the short term by increasing soil organic matter and water infiltration if they don't outcompete desirable vegetation. Finally, you may choose to screen out views of problematic species with more desirable ones. You'll worry less about what you can't see.

Desert plant communities follow a different pattern of succession than compared to wetter climates. Extreme droughts, for instance, can quickly change vegetation, but the recruitment of species after that event is slower in deserts than in wetter areas. Many native perennials and shrubs regenerate after disturbance or stress, allowing the plant community to skip a step of succession. The same characters return to the stage without a warm-up act. In one sense, desert plant communities are entangled mosaics of plants that evolved from many ongoing episodes of stress and disturbance. While annual species in more temperate areas generally only occur in response to disturbance, desert ecosystems feature ruderals throughout their life stages. The abundance of these species is often directly linked to annual precipitation and favorable temperatures during the fall and winter months that favor germination.

The rugged character of a dead sumac (Rhus) scaffolding this steppe-inspired meadow at Denver Botanic Gardens (Denver, Colorado, US) speaks volumes of the inherent ruggedness of the region's landscapes.

Steppes

Steppes are expansive, grass- and shrub-dominated landscapes emblematic of vast, open areas in central Asia, Eastern Europe, central and western North America, and the South American Patagonia. Most steppes occur as a function of climate in transitions between other charismatic and often more easily defined ecoregions like deserts, Mediterranean zones, and maritime provinces. Curiously, mountains are always involved.

The ecology of steppe regions is a study of resilience and adaptation, a mosaic of possibilities that informs good planting and gardening decisions. Forging a relationship with this place and its plants isn't for the faint of heart. Superblooms and rampant growth flourish in years of abundance, a spectacle to remember when harsh conditions return. Gardening in steppe regions deals with these limitations by definition, embracing ecologically imposed stress as a prerequisite.

The steppe climate, marked by extreme temperature fluctuations and low rainfall, shapes a resilient, enduring plant palette with unique adaptations. These species evolved to coexist with the sporadic disturbances of grazing and wildfire, contributing to the steppe's intricate ecological tapestry. Seasonally challenged by aridity, soils demand careful consideration of water management and plant selection. Acknowledging these conditions allows gardeners to harmonize their efforts with the steppe's natural rhythm, fostering a garden that is a testament to the region's stark beauty.

Site Conditions

Steppe regions generally receive less than 20 inches (51 cm) of annual precipitation, although the timing and form depend greatly on geography. Steppe soils, like deserts, tend to be alkaline and rich in minerals, which belies the depauperate appearance of much of the region's vegetation. They can vary dramatically due to the

North American steppe natives like Cucurbita foetidissima *(stinking cucumber) grow from a thick, starchy caudiciform structure that ensures long-term viability in a challenging environment.*

underlying differences in geology associated with mountain or plateau development. Given the limited vegetation, these soils sit exposed near the surface, leading to further chemistry and structure variation.

Microclimates present enviable opportunities for site-specific gardening in steppe regions, the variation of which can produce unfolding tapestries of seemingly unrelated plants within short distances. Cold canyon walls harbor shade-dwelling ferns and species clinging to their westernmost outpost, odd cohorts to yuccas, and wind-pruned shrubs lining the hillside above. Survey your landscape for these situations, often informed by reflective heat from rocks but also by aspects and thermal masses of buildings and trees. Microclimates formed by variations in soil composition—for example, the presence of selenium or thick layers of limestone, clay, marl, and gypsum—immediately define the planting palettes you can use. Understanding these ground rules saves headaches later.

Human disturbance has introduced the same challenges to the extant landscape in these regions as others. Heavy soil compaction impounds the natural movement of water through the vertical soil column. Even in a small landscape, these challenges can pose hurdles for home gardeners working to develop durable, resilient plant communities. Where water can't drain readily, it either drains slowly or evaporates, leaving behind mineral deposits that affect the soil horizon where most plant roots exist. Disturbances like these can also create novel opportunities for introduced, non-native species to establish and spread. The presence of these species may complicate the site dynamics, shifting where water flows and how organic matter accumulates.

Light intensity plays a crucial role in gardening within steppe regions, where the expansive, open landscapes receive abundant, glaring sunlight throughout the year. Plants native to these areas are uniquely adapted to harness the intense light, often with inclined leaf arrangements, enabling them to withstand the harsh environment and conserve water. Additionally, understanding the nuances of light intensity throughout the day and seasons can help inform garden layouts.

Planting

The word *xeriscape* occupies new cultural meaning in steppe regions as municipalities emphasize the value of water conservation in residential landscapes. Mapping the water flow across your site can give you clues about where to invest in its conservation and adapt plantings to match. These so-called "hydrozones" may span the gamut of water needs or availability. Ecologically speaking, if you must irrigate it to keep it alive, why are you planting it as part of a resilient plant community?

Steppe species reflect the strain of their environment with rugged constitutions capable of seemingly magical feats like rebounding from desiccating winds, resprouting after pounding hail, and resurging from untimely frosts. The gestalt plant palette, maximally arrayed, conveys the breadth and diversity of stress responses: fierce agaves, sky-bound yuccas, smoke-like grasses, and low-growing succulents.

Grasses dominate the visual aesthetic of most steppe environments. While they reign with abundance, grasses aren't alone in their prominence. Steppes often feature robust shrub communities, a central

Steppe plantings feature dramatic textures conveyed by the stark contrasts in growth habits of plants adapted to the region. Planting design by Kevin Philip Williams, Denver Botanic Garden (Denver, Colorado, US).

organizing element visually and ecologically. In an increasingly warmer world, these communities will flourish as woody C4 plants expand their territory beyond historical bounds. Translating this idea to a horticultural landscape is viable, provided you mind the players' habits, which may excel even more with additional garden-scale resources (i.e., water). Enlisting the help of rugged herbaceous perennials rounds out the plant palette, especially when they offer strong textural contrasts to grasses and shrubs.

Emphasizing the natural rhythms of the steppe ensures a garden that is both sustainable and reflective of the region's unique ecological character. In stressful environments, planting diversely has functional benefits. High-diversity plant communities cope with stress cooperatively and thrive on the shoulders of the most stress-resistant species. When times are lean, the aesthetic and ecological functions rest on these bedrock contributions. As you consider planting schemes in this biome, lean into these species that persist against all odds.

No plant is drought-tolerant unless established, a hard lesson many learn from trial and error. The watering needs of plants after installation could stretch beyond available supplies. Plan new projects based on the greatest seasonal water availability or work in phases to avoid consumptive splurging.

Management and Stewardship

Perhaps more so than any other biome treatment in this book, the plantings in steppe climates succeed or fail based on their fitness to place. Steppe gardens revel in openness framed by yawning horizons and big skies, both sources of environmental stress. Rocks or underlying geology are never far away, either. Inside these demanding and harsh frames, rugged plants live intricately beautiful lives, the antithesis of lushness but no less rich. These plants look like they belong here, with thin leaves and pliable stems in shades of gray, green, and blue that reflect sunlight and minimize desiccation. Plants have evolved with considerable amplitude to environmental stress in regions where aridity is the norm. Adopt them as ready partners.

Over many years, successful steppe gardens thrive from an understanding of how water accumulates and moves through the garden environment. While you may undertake inventive means of catching and storing water, observing how it travels at the surface will inform just as much.

Managing organic matter in steppe gardens depends on the precedent condition. In steppe regions with fertile soils, called *chernozems*, diverse plant communities produce abundant biomass, which, if allowed to decompose, recharge the soil with new organic inputs. In leaner steppe regions, a gardener may have to resist gilding the scene lest a planting starts to look transplanted from somewhere else. In urban settings, you may inherit little underfoot that would improve your success. Cooperating with this leanness, like that which you might encounter in a new construction environment, may prove more durable in the long run if you can establish a stress-tolerant planting. Gravel and crevice gardens offer novel ways of establishing plants in these settings.

In contrast to meadows and prairies, steppe-inspired plantings produce less biomass. Limited by a short season, intense light, and perhaps lean soils, plants don't grow as much as they would in wealthier circumstances. For the gardener, this modesty pays off in having less to contend with at the outset of spring. In natural ecosystems, this annual cutting would happen with the teeth of herbivores, who flock to green pastures once the snow melts. In the horticultural setting, sharpening the blades of your mower or hand shears makes quick work as you nimbly navigate tussocks of grasses, spiny shrubs, and succulent rosettes.

Acclaimed landscape designer Lauren Springer's approach is rooted in a water-conscious ethos, as shown in the Undaunted Garden at the Gardens on Spring Creek (Fort Collins, Colorado, US).

Research conducted in steppe grasslands shows that droughts cause more stress to plant communities with lower levels of plant diversity. In regions with historically less plant diversity and extreme annual precipitation regimes, such as steppes and mid-continental grasslands, these effects will likely only become more pronounced with climate change. Plant communities in these regions will adapt and respond in real-time but may shift in composition as extreme events alter the roster of species. Garden environments often buffer against extreme stress: you can decide to water during an extreme drought, even just a few times, to protect your investment. If you don't and some plants die over time, you can always replace or substitute them. Either strategy—watering or replanting—illustrates a short-term, life-supporting dynamic that can have near- and long-term implications for biodiversity at the garden scale.

The Best Tools for Ecological Gardening

Everyone has their tools of choice. Tools make gardening easier, if not more effective. Like kitchen utensils and equipment, more gadgets abound than reasons to own them. Stick to the most essential implements and keep them in good working order. I organized my favorites around their function with an emphasis on hand tools. The only machine in our garden is a pushable lawnmower fitted with mulching blades, which appears in early spring for cutting back the meadows and occasionally trimming the paths in summer. As you do a similar inventory, consider what you need tools for and then seek out the most comfortable options. You may add categories as the workings of your place require.

Digging

If you follow the mantra "just keep planting," you'll need an adequately shaped blade attached to a good handle to match your planting size. I prefer to dig many small holes instead of large ones of any number. I'm partial to a perennial spade about as long as my arm, especially those manufactured by Sneeboer in the Netherlands. The handle length means I can use it with one arm, deftly notching the soil at a depth to match the pot I'm working with. Hand trowels are valuable, too, provided the blades remain sharp and clean. Hundreds of styles, shapes, and brands abound, with various improvements for handling and grip. I have a half dozen in the garden shed and regularly use one. A garden knife, or *hori hori*, ranks high on the lists of many gardeners as a versatile tool for many purposes. You may choose this over a trowel simply because of its flexibility. A round-headed spade or garden fork helps turn soil and break up compacted areas. The latter also comes in handy for larger pots, including trees and shrubs.

Pruning and Cutting

Pruning and cutting require well-maintained blades to keep the work efficient and plants healthy. You need one or a couple of good pairs of bypass pruners (secateurs) so you can leave one in the garden and still have one in the tool bin. As branch diameter increases, scale the tool accordingly with loppers or pruning saws depending on how much pole length you need to reach whatever you're cutting. A pole saw may be necessary for higher branches and limbs, mainly as canopies mature.

Weeding and Disturbance

Your two hands, provided you have at least one, are the most intelligent tools for weeding. However, lunging to the ground to serve justice on the species you wish to control is tiresome, particularly with age. A sharp hoe on a handle long enough not to require stooping comes in handy more than once a year. Inventors have conjured up endless iterations, altering the head's shape, size, and orientation. Whichever you choose, opt for the version that introduces only as much disturbance as is necessary to kill your target (which requires knowing how it grows and how long its roots are). Maiming weeds only leads to more work, which, at any rate, accumulates readily when controlling plant life. Apart from weeding, which is plenty disturbing, some tools primarily serve a role in disturbing the surface of the ground. At least two rakes should hang in your shed, one for leveling soil and the other for piling up organic matter.

Keeping Up with Rain

I grew up on a farm, so keeping track of rainfall comes naturally to me. I like to know when it happened and track how much the garden received, which is valuable data for approximating when I need to water again and supplying small talk when asked about the weather. A digital rain gauge mounted near the rain barrel works well. A rain barrel may not have much use in dry years if rain never falls to fill it. In years of abundance, it lowers the water bill. Few are so attractive that you would want to look at them often, but a handful of companies have pioneered textured finishes in a noble attempt to improve the aesthetic.

Epilogue

"Perhaps the gardener is not someone who makes forms survive over time, but over time, if possible, ensures that enchantment survives."
—Gilles Clément in *The Planetary Garden*

In the driven, growth-oriented world we live in, you might wonder how to define success in the natural garden. As you look out over your parcel, sweat pooling on your brow after a long afternoon in midsummer, what gives you satisfaction and confidence that you're playing a relevant part in the nature of your place? How do you know if your natural garden has made a difference?

Some years ago, in much the same moment, I realized that what I took pride or pleasure in was often not of my doing. Nature happened despite my exertion. My labors—that careful plant combination near the entrance to the meadow or the exacting placement of shrubs in the hedgerow—were least likely to predict where and how nature came into view. After all, no amount of toil brings more ground-nesting bees or bark-encrusting lichens to the garden. Unbeknownst to you, they may have found bare earth or exposed beams near the foundation of your garden shed. Just don't get in the way.

Imagine for a moment what success *could* look like. Imagine your neighborhood and its landscapes in the future. Gardens form an interconnected patchwork of mostly native plants, at least those that still thrive in a warmer world, alongside the novel environments cropping up in our remnant greenspaces and parklands. People accept the challenges of mosaic landscapes that remain as artifacts from a more ecologically disruptive period of human history. Given the alternatives, verdancy is the better option. Gardeners take passion in finding an amenable balance of life, identity, and culture. Your neighbor still doesn't like yellow flowers, but they still plant densely and diversely, cohabitating with local nature in their own idiosyncratic way. Another neighbor down the street plants a few more trees and shrubs every year, preferring to invest their time in pruning and harvesting rather than growing many herbaceous perennials. Their lawn is an understory matrix of sedges and ground-covers mown once a year. The most marvelous thing about this future neighborhood is that each patch looks a little different than the next one, a teeming mosaic of diverse, ecosystem services. These gardens aren't once-and-future arks but rather complex habitats that take shape from a cascade of natural, if not human-mediated processes. These gardeners play the same game, but the rules aren't so rigid as to tally a score of who is winning or losing, doing better or worse. The rules are quite simple; the players remain in the game.

◀ *Small home gardens should be places of enchantment and ecology as demonstrated here in this place-driven, plant-rich home garden in Denver, Colorado, US. Planting and gardening by Mike Kintgen.*

I want to imagine such a hopeful future, even if I'm sobered by reality. Absent another degree or advanced study, you probably won't undertake a complete census of the life in your garden (although I won't discourage you if the idea takes root). Maybe you'll set a goal to learn the names of the birds you see in a given year. To name something is to begin to understand it. Perhaps you'll share your experiences with friends or social organizations. You could just host a garden party and normalize a natural garden lifestyle. You may find that success isn't merely a result but the respect and collaboration that accompanies the experience.

Striking a balance between short-term and long-term goals can ensure sustained success. What you measure in the early years of planting won't and shouldn't be the same as what you measure in a more established landscape. Success in ecological gardening extends beyond beauty and biomass. Your natural garden isn't a fourth-quarter earnings report—it's not measured by output or production in a single year. Success is a relationship you develop with the place, the sincerity of your intentions, the knowledge you share, the environment you respect, and the joy you find when plants thrive.

There's an old quote that goes: "If you stumble, make it part of the dance." You'll learn plenty of new dance moves in the natural garden. The capacity to adapt and alter strategies should be a fundamental aspect of your gardening experience. As with nature, change is constant, and flexibility is key to thriving with it. If you take plenty of photos, you'll also look back and realize that even at the peak of your perceived failings, you were better off than you knew. Few other creatures on the planet suffer their own metacognition in the way we do, a curious consequence of our evolution. Consider all that is animal about your puttering, planting, and plucking. Gardening in stewardship to place is a higher-order ecological aspiration with selfish and communal benefits.

I hope by now you have plenty of reason to discard the tiresome yarn about natural gardens lacking joy and pleasure. Natural gardens offer a steady dopamine drip, a daily cascade of pleasure, satisfaction, motivation, and reward for being consciously part of something, whether you can name every creature that walks through your garden or not. After all, you don't wake up one morning and decide to interact with the world through your natural garden. You wake up and realize you have a choice for *how* to show up in a garden that's already a part of the world.

October in the Long Look Prairie, Three Oaks Garden (Des Moines, Iowa, US).

Glossary for the Ecological Gardener

As with any practice, a lexicon describes the work and how it's done. Curated from many years of frequently asked questions, here is a concise collection of relevant terminology, arranged alphabetically, for natural gardening.

Abundance: The relative representation of a species in a particular ecosystem or habitat.

Bioregion: A geographical territory defined by ecosystems or unique combinations of flora, fauna, geology, climate, and watersheds. Bioregions are often considered a more holistic way to view and manage the environment because they encompass entire ecosystems, including interactions with human inhabitants. Bioregions generally comprise several ecoregions (see below).

Competition: The interaction between organisms or species in which the presence of another lowers the fitness of one.

Cooperation: The process where groups of organisms work or act together for common or mutual benefits.

Cultivar: A plant variety that has originated and persisted under cultivation.

Disturbance: An event that changes a community, removing organisms and altering resource availability. At an individual plant population level, disturbance results in a partial or total loss of biomass, often arising from the activities of herbivores, pathogens, and humans. Disturbance is generally episodic, as in the case of extreme weather, frosts, or fire.

Ecoregion: A geographically defined area containing distinct communities of plants, animals, and other organisms. These communities interact with the physical environment distinctly, creating a specific habitat identified by analyzing patterns including geology, vegetation, climate, soils, land use, wildlife, and hydrology.

Ecotype: A genetically distinct geographic variety, population, or race within a species adapted to specific environmental conditions. The phrase *local ecotype* is well-established in practice but carries more rhetorical than empirical weight. Using plants from localities adjacent to restorations arose in mid-twentieth-century ecological practices but has little support on its merits from the scientific literature. For broadly distributed plant species, there are often few appreciable genetic or ecological differences in populations within a few hundred miles of each other, although the effect is taxon-specific. Regardless, ecological practices shouldn't be founded on a poorly resolved blanket distinction.

Evenness: A measure of the relative abundance of different species making up the richness of an area.

Forbs: Herbaceous flowering plants that are not grasses, sedges, or rushes.

Generalist: An ecological strategy that enables organisms or species to thrive in various environmental conditions and utilize diverse resources. Generalists are inherently flexible in diet and habitat preferences, adapting to different environmental conditions. Generalists hold the world together, amplifying the nestedness of natural communities by showing up everywhere. Contrast with specialists.

Genotype: The genetic constitution of an individual organism.

Herbivory: The eating of plants by animals.

Hybrid: A cultivar that results from crossing two different varieties or species. Hybrids cannot typically be reproduced through seed but must be propagated through asexual means such as cuttings, grafting, or tissue culture.

Invasive Plant: A plant that is not native to a specific location and tends to spread to a degree that causes damage to the environment, human economy, or human health. Invasive plants are a small but troublesome subcategory of naturalized plants.

Matrix: In the traditional ecology literature, this term refers to the background ecological system or environment in which communities, ecosystems, or species are embedded. In plantings, we adapt that term to refer to the primary layer of vegetation closest to the ground, which is generally abundant throughout the design.

Nativar: A portmanteau of "native" and "cultivar" referring to a cultivated selection of a native plant species.

Native Plant: A plant that occurs naturally in a region, ecosystem, or habitat without human introduction (i.e., indigenous beyond human timescales). The quality of being native requires context and should always be used with a geographic qualifier to define the scope of its meaning precisely.

Naturalized Plant: A non-native plant adapted to an area and maintains reproductively viable populations without direct human intervention.

Non-native Plant: A plant that occurs in a region that is not historically native; often introduced by humans. Without reproduction, many non-native plants cannot persist beyond the envelope of human activities. The quality of being nonnative requires context and should always be used with a geographic qualifier to define the scope of its meaning precisely.

Novel Ecosystem: An ecosystem that consists of new combinations of species that have not previously coexisted, often due to human activity.

Open-pollinated: Cultivars that result from pollination by insects, birds, wind, or human hands and produce offspring true to the parent plant. Heirloom cultivars are often old, open-pollinated varieties passed through cultural generations, usually due to horticulturally valued characteristics.

Plant Community: A collection of plant species within a designated geographical area that interact with each other and their environment.

Provenance: The geographical origin or source of a plant or seed. In horticultural terms, the word is sometimes used to indicate where germplasm was initially collected or produced.

Resilience: The capacity of an ecosystem to withstand or absorb disturbances while maintaining its fundamental structure, functions, and processes. A resilient ecosystem resists major changes due to disturbance or during its recovery.

Restoration: The process of assisting the recovery of an ecosystem that has been degraded, damaged, or destroyed to a stable condition by actively managing the environment and reintroducing native species. Contrast with rewilding.

Rewilding: A conservation effort focused on restoring natural processes, even when specific ecological functions are accomplished by organisms without historical precedents. The goal of rewilding is to let natural processes reorganize landscapes given contemporary conditions and disturbances through strategies like reintroducing megafauna, predators, and climate-adapted species regardless of origin. Rewilded landscapes ultimately exist with minimal human intervention. Contrast with restoration.

Ruderal: A plant species that colonizes landscapes after disturbance; synonymous with pioneer species.

Specialist: An ecological strategy of highly adapted organisms or species to occupy a narrow niche, often shaped by a preference for food or habitat.

Species Richness: The number of species represented in an ecological community, landscape, or region.

Stress: An environmental condition that restricts plant productivity, such as the shortage of light, water, nutrients, or extreme temperatures. Stresses are generally features of landscape settings but can exist on both short- and long-term timescales.

Structure: Architectural plants or plant communities with distinctive shapes, forms, or textures that contribute to the overall visual infrastructure of a garden or landscape. These plants are typically used sparingly and strategically for maximum impact, often serving as the backbone around which other plantings are arranged. They help to create a sense of order and coherence in the garden, guiding the eye and often providing year-round interest.

Vignettes: Distinct areas or scenes, often used in planting design to describe seasonally dynamic patterns or layers within a habitat or garden setting that offer a particular view or experience.

References

Abella, Scott R. 2017. "Restoring Desert Ecosystems." In *Routledge Handbook of Ecological and Environmental Restoration*, edited by Stuart K. Allison and Stephen D. Murphy, 1st ed., 158–72. London; New York: Routledge. https://doi.org/10.4324/9781315685977.

Andermann, Tobias, Alexandre Antonelli, Russell L. Barrett, and Daniele Silvestro. 2022. "Estimating Alpha, Beta, and Gamma Diversity Through Deep Learning." *Frontiers in Plant Science* 13 (April): 839407. https://doi.org/10.3389/fpls.2022.839407.

Anderson, Max, Ellen L. Rotheray, and Fiona Mathews. 2023. "Marvellous Moths! Pollen Deposition Rate of Bramble (*Rubus futicosus* L. agg.) Is Greater at Night than Day." *PLoS ONE* 18 (3): e0281810. https://doi.org/10.1371/journal.pone.0281810.

Anthony, Mark A., S. Franz Bender, and Marcel G. A. van der Heijden. 2023. "Enumerating Soil Biodiversity." *Proceedings of the National Academy of Sciences of the United States of America* 120 (33): e2304663120. https://doi.org/10.1073/pnas.2304663120.

Berry, Wendell, and Norman Wirzba. 2002. *The Art of the Commonplace: The Agrarian Essays of Wendell Berry*. Washington, DC: Shoemaker & Hoard.

Berthon, Katherine, Freya Thomas, and Sarah Bekessy. 2021. "The Role of 'Nativeness' in Urban Greening to Support Animal Biodiversity." *Landscape and Urban Planning* 205 (January): 103959. https://doi.org/10.1016/j.landurbplan.2020.103959.

Biella, Paolo, Asma Akter, Jeff Ollerton, Sam Tarrant, Štěpán Janeček, Jana Jersáková, and Jan Klecka. 2019. "Experimental Loss of Generalist Plants Reveals Alterations in Plant-Pollinator Interactions and a Constrained Flexibility of Foraging." *Scientific Reports* 9 (1): 7376. https://doi.org/10.1038/s41598-019-43553-4.

Braschler, Brigitte, José D. Gilgado, Valerie Zwahlen, Hans-Peter Rusterholz, Sascha Buchholz, and Bruno Baur. 2020. "Ground-Dwelling Invertebrate Diversity in Domestic Gardens along a Rural-Urban Gradient: Landscape Characteristics Are More Important than Garden Characteristics." *PLoS ONE* 15 (10): e0240061. https://doi.org/10.1371/journal.pone.0240061.

Breitschopf, Eva, and Kari Anne Bråthen. 2023. "Perception and Appreciation of Plant Biodiversity among Experts and Laypeople." *People and Nature* 5 (2): 826–38. https://doi.org/10.1002/pan3.10455.

Bren d'Amour, Christopher, Femke Reitsma, Giovanni Baiocchi, Stephan Barthel, Burak Güneralp, Karl-Heinz Erb, Helmut Haberl, Felix Creutzig, and Karen C. Seto. 2017. "Future Urban Land Expansion and Implications for Global Croplands." *Proceedings of the National Academy of Sciences of the United States of America* 114 (34): 8939–44. https://doi.org/10.1073/pnas.1606036114.

Cane, James H., Robert Minckley, Linda Kervin, and T'Ai Roulston. 2005. "Temporally Persistent Patterns of Incidence and Abundance in a Pollinator Guild at Annual and Decadal Scales: The Bees of Larrea Tridentata" *Biological Journal of the Linnean Society* 85 (3): 319–29. https://doi.org/10.1111/j.1095-8312.2005.00502.x.

Carse, James P. 1986. *Finite and Infinite Games*. New York: Free Press.

Clément, Gilles. 2015. *"The Planetary Garden" and Other Writings*. Philadelphia: University of Pennsylvania Press.

Cronon, William, ed. 1996. *Uncommon Ground: Rethinking the Human Place in Nature*. Paperback ed. New York, NY: W.W. Norton & Co.

Delahay, Richard J., D. Sherman, B. Soyalan, and K. J. Gaston. 2023. "Biodiversity in Residential Gardens: A Review of the Evidence Base." *Biodiversity and Conservation* 32 (13): 4155–79. https://doi.org/10.1007/s10531-023-02694-9.

du Toit, Johan T. du, and Nathalie Pettorelli. 2019. "The Differences between Rewilding and Restoring an Ecologically Degraded Landscape." *Journal of Applied Ecology* 56 (11): 2467–71. https://doi.org/10.1111/1365-2664.13487.

Dutton, G. F. 1997. *Some Branch against the Sky: The Practice and Principles of Marginal Gardening*. Newton Abbot, [England]: Portland, OR: David & Charles; Timber Press.

Elkin, Rosetta S. 2022. *Plant Life: The Entangled Politics of Afforestation*. Minneapolis: University of Minnesota Press.

Erickson, E, R. R. Junker, J. G. Ali, N McCartney, H. M. Patch, and C. M. Grozinger. 2022. "Complex Floral Traits Shape Pollinator Attraction to Ornamental Plants." *Annals of Botany* 130 (4): 561–77. https://doi.org/10.1093/aob/mcac082.

Franco, José Tomás. 2023. "Native Forests, the Landscaping That Cities Need." *ArchDaily*. April 4, 2023. https://www.archdaily.com/998848/native-forests-the-landscaping-that-cities-need.

Frankie, Gordon, Ingrid Feng, Robbin Thorp, Jaime Pawelek, Marissa Helene Chase, Christopher C. Jadallah, and Mark Rizzardi. 2019. "Native and Non-Native Plants Attract Diverse Bees to Urban Gardens in California." *Journal of Pollination Ecology* 25 (May). https://doi.org/10.26786/1920-7603(2019)505.

Georgi, Maria M., Stefanie M. Gärtner, Marc I. Förschler, Jörn Buse, Felix Fornoff, Axel Ssymank, Yvonne Oelmann, and Alexandra-Maria Klein. 2023. "Mulching Time of Forest Meadows Influences Insect Diversity." *Insect Conservation and Diversity* 16 (3): 368–78. https://doi.org/10.1111/icad.12629.

Gerritsen, Henk. 2014. *Essay on Gardening*. Translated by Mark Speer. Amsterdam: Architectura & Natura Press.

Glenn, Joshua, and Rob Walker, eds. 2012. *Significant Objects*. Seattle, WA: Fantagraphics Books.

Gobster, Paul H., Joan I. Nassauer, Terry C. Daniel, and Gary Fry. 2007. "The Shared Landscape: What Does Aesthetics Have to Do with Ecology?" *Landscape Ecology* 22 (7): 959–72. https://doi.org/10.1007/s10980-007-9110-x.

Golden, James. 2022. View from Federal Twist: *A New Way of Thinking about Gardens, Nature and Ourselves*. London: Filbert Press.

Hall, Damon M., Gerardo R. Camilo, Rebecca K. Tonietto, Jeff Ollerton, Karin Ahrné, Mike Arduser, John S. Ascher, et al. 2017. "The City as a Refuge for Insect Pollinators." *Conservation Biology* 31 (1): 24–29. https://doi.org/10.1111/cobi.12840.

Harker, Donald F., ed. 1993. *Landscape Restoration Handbook*. Boca Raton, FL: Lewis Publishers.

Hoyle, Helen, James Hitchmough, and Anna Jorgensen. 2017. "All about the 'Wow Factor'? The Relationships between Aesthetics, Restorative Effect and Perceived Biodiversity in Designed Urban Planting." *Landscape and Urban Planning* 164 (August): 109–23. https://doi.org/10.1016/j.landurbplan.2017.03.011.

Huang, Yuanyuan, Gideon Stein, Olaf Kolle, Karl Kübler, Ernst-Detlef Schulze, Hui Dong, David Eichenberg, et al. 2023. "Enhanced Stability of Grassland Soil Temperature by Plant Diversity." *Nature Geoscience*, 17 (December): 44-50. https://doi.org/10.1038/s41561-023-01338-5.

Jackson, John Brinckerhoff. 1984. *Discovering the Vernacular Landscape*. New Haven, CT: Yale University Press.

Karson, Robin S., Jane Roy Brown, Sarah Allaback, and Library of American Landscape History, eds. 2017. *Warren H. Manning, Landscape Architect and Environmental Planner*. Critical Perspectives in the History of Environmental Design. Amherst, MA: Athens, Georgia: Library of American Landscape History; University of Georgia Press.

King, Rachel A., Jamie Pullen, Susan C. Cook-Patton, and John D. Parker. 2023. "Diversity Stabilizes but Does Not Increase Sapling Survival in a Tree Diversity Experiment." *Restoration Ecology* 31 (5): e13927. https://doi.org/10.1111/rec.13927.

Kingsbury, Noel. 2011. *Hybrid: The History and Science of Plant Breeding*. Chicago, IL: University of Chicago Press. https://press.uchicago.edu/ucp/books/book/chicago/H/bo5387732.html.

Koštál, Vladimír. 2006. "Eco-Physiological Phases of Insect Diapause." *Journal of Insect Physiology* 52 (2): 113–27. https://doi.org/10.1016/j.jinsphys.2005.09.008.

Langellotto, Gail A., and Robert F. Denno. 2004. "Responses of Invertebrate Natural Enemies to Complex-Structured Habitats: A Meta-Analytical Synthesis." *Oecologia* 139 (April): 1–10. https://doi.org/10.1007/s00442-004-1497-3.

Liira, J., and I. Jürjendal. 2023. "Are Bees Attracted by Flower Richness? Implications for Ecosystem Service-Based Policy." *Ecological Indicators* 154 (October): 110927. https://doi.org/10.1016/j.ecolind.2023.110927.

Loram, Alison, Jamie Tratalos, Philip H. Warren, and Kevin J. Gaston. 2007. "Urban Domestic Gardens (X): The Extent & Structure of the Resource in Five Major Cities." *Landscape Ecology* 22 (January): 601–15. https://doi.org/10.1007/s10980-006-9051-9.

Ma, Qin, Yanjun Su, Chunyue Niu, Qin Ma, Tianyu Hu, Xiangzhong Luo, Xiaonan Tai, et al. 2023. "Tree Mortality during Long-Term Droughts Is Lower in Structurally Complex Forest Stands." *Nature Communications* 14 (1): 7467. https://doi.org/10.1038/s41467-023-43083-8.

Marris, Emma. 2013. *Rambunctious Garden: Saving Nature in a Post-Wild World*. Paperback ed. New York: Bloomsbury Publishing.

Matteson, Kevin C., and Gail A. Langellotto. 2011. "Small Scale Additions of Native Plants Fail to Increase Beneficial Insect Richness in Urban Gardens." *Insect Conservation and Diversity* 4 (2): 89–98. https://doi.org/10.1111/j.1752-4598.2010.00103.x.

Morrison, Darrel G. 2021. *Beauty of the Wild: A Life Designing Landscapes Inspired by Nature*. Amherst, MA: Library of American Landscape History.

Mumaw, Laura. 2017. "Transforming Urban Gardeners into Land Stewards." *Journal of Environmental Psychology* 52 (October): 92–103. https://doi.org/10.1016/j.jenvp.2017.05.003.

Nassauer, Joan Iverson. 1995. "Messy Ecosystems, Orderly Frames." *Landscape Journal* 14 (2): 161–70.

Nassauer, Joan Iverson. 2012. "Landscape as Method and Medium for the Ecological Design of Cities." In *Resilience in Ecology and Urban Design: Linking Theory and Practice for Sustainable Cities*, ed. Pickett, S., Cadenasso, M., and McGrath, B. 79–98. Springer.

Nelson, Mykl, Gwynne Mhuireach, and Gail A. Langellotto. 2022. "Excess Fertility in Residential-Scale Urban Agriculture Soils in Two Western Oregon Cities, USA." *Urban Agriculture & Regional Food Systems* 7 (1): e20027. https://doi.org/10.1002/uar2.20027.

Pearce, Fred. 2015. *The New Wild: Why Invasive Species Will Be Nature's Salvation*. Boston, MA: Beacon Press.

Pearse, William D., Jeannine Cavender-Bares, Sarah E. Hobbie, Meghan L. Avolio, Neil Bettez, Rinku Roy Chowdhury, Lindsay E. Darling, et al. 2018. "Homogenization of Plant Diversity, Composition, and Structure in North American Urban Yards." *Ecosphere* 9 (2): e02105. https://doi.org/10.1002/ecs2.2105.

Philpott, Stacy M., Julie Cotton, Peter Bichier, Russell L. Friedrich, Leigh C. Moorhead, Shinsuke Uno, and Monica Valdez. 2014. "Local and Landscape Drivers of Arthropod Abundance, Richness, and Trophic Composition in Urban Habitats." *Urban Ecosystems* 17 (2): 513–32. https://doi.org/10.1007/s11252-013-0333-0.

Pope, Nori, and Sandra Pope. 1998. *Color by Design: Planting the Contemporary Garden*. San Francisco, CA: SOMA Books.

Ray, C. Claiborne. 2011. "As Old as Dirt." *The New York Times*, June 13, 2011, sec. Science. https://www.nytimes.com/2011/06/14/science/14qna.html.

Schilling, Keith E., and Pauline Drobney. 2014. "Hydrologic Recovery with Prairie Reconstruction at Neal Smith National Wildlife Refuge, Jasper County, Iowa." U.S. Fish and Wildlife Service.

Smallidge, Peter J., Brett Chedzoy, Paul Curtis, and Katherine Sims. 2021. "Evaluating the Construction and Effectiveness of Slash Walls at the Perimeter of Regeneration Harvests to Exclude Deer." *Forest Ecology and Management* 497 (October): 119529. https://doi.org/10.1016/j.foreco.2021.119529.

Smith, Melinda D., Kate D. Wilkins, Martin C. Holdrege, Peter Wilfahrt, Scott L. Collins, Alan K. Knapp, Osvaldo E. Sala, et al. 2024. "Extreme Drought Impacts Have Been Underestimated in Grasslands and Shrublands Globally." *Proceedings of the National Academy of Sciences of the United States of America* 121 (4): e2309881120. https://doi.org/10.1073/pnas.2309881120.

't Zandt, Dina in, Zuzana Kolaříková, Tomáš Cajthaml, and Zuzana Münzbergová. 2023. "Plant Community Stability Is Associated with a Decoupling of Prokaryote and Fungal Soil Networks." *Nature Communications* 14 (1): 3736. https://doi.org/10.1038/s41467-023-39464-8.

Tew, Nicholas E., Katherine C. R. Baldock, Ian P. Vaughan, Stephanie Bird, and Jane Memmott. 2022. "Turnover in Floral Composition Explains Species Diversity and Temporal Stability in the Nectar Supply of Urban Residential Gardens." *Journal of Applied Ecology* 59 (3): 801–11. https://doi.org/10.1111/1365-2664.14094.

Tree, Isabella, and Charlie Burrell. 2023. *The Book of Wilding: A Practical Guide to Rewilding Big and Small*. London: Bloomsbury Publishing.

Tresch, Simon, David Frey, Renée-Claire Le Bayon, Paul Mäder, Bernhard Stehle, Andreas Fliessbach, and Marco Moretti. 2019. "Direct and Indirect Effects of Urban Gardening on Aboveground and Belowground Diversity Influencing Soil Multifunctionality." *Scientific Reports* 9 (1): 9769. https://doi.org/10.1038/s41598-019-46024-y.

Tully, Kate, and Rebecca Ryals. 2017. "Nutrient Cycling in Agroecosystems: Balancing Food and Environmental Objectives." *Agroecology and Sustainable Food Systems* 41 (7): 761–98. https://doi.org/10.1080/21683565.2017.1336149.

Wallington, Jack. 2019. *Wild about Weeds: Garden Design with Rebel Plants*. London: Laurence King Publishing.

Warner, Emily, Susan C. Cook-Patton, Owen T. Lewis, Nick Brown, Julia Koricheva, Nico Eisenhauer, Olga Ferlian, et al. 2023. "Young Mixed Planted Forests Store More Carbon than Monocultures—a Meta-Analysis." *Frontiers in Forests and Global Change* 6. https://www.frontiersin.org/articles/10.3389/ffgc.2023.1226514.

Wei, Xinzeng, Yaozhan Xu, Linyu Lyu, Zhiqiang Xiao, Shitong Wang, Teng Yang, and Mingxi Jiang. 2023. "Impacts of Ecological Restoration on the Genetic Diversity of Plant Species: A Global Meta-Analysis." *Journal of Applied Ecology* 60 (6): 1149–60. https://doi.org/10.1111/1365-2664.14390.

Werner, Chhaya M., Truman P. Young, and Katharine L. Stuble. 2024. "Year Effects Drive Beta Diversity, but Unevenly across Plant Community Types." *Ecology* 105 (1): e4188. https://doi.org/10.1002/ecy.4188.

Wintle, Brendan A., Heini Kujala, Amy Whitehead, Alison Cameron, Sam Veloz, Aija Kukkala, Atte Moilanen, et al. 2019. "Global Synthesis of Conservation Studies Reveals the Importance of Small Habitat Patches for Biodiversity." *Proceedings of the National Academy of Sciences of the United States of America* 116 (3): 909–14. https://doi.org/10.1073/pnas.1813051115.

Wolschke-Bulmahn, Joachim. 1997. *Nature and Ideology: Nature and Garden Design in the Twentieth Century.* Washington, DC: Dumbarton Oaks, Trustees for Harvard University. http://archive.org/details/wolschke-bulmahn-nature-and-ideology.

Wood, Eric M., and Sevan Esaian. 2020. "The Importance of Street Trees to Urban Avifauna." *Ecological Applications* 30 (7): e02149. https://doi.org/10.1002/eap.2149.

Wrinkle, Louise Agee. 2017. *Listen to the Land: Creating a Southern Woodland Garden.* Birmingham, AL: Birmingham Home and Garden: PMT Publishing.

About the Author

Kelly D. Norris is a leading American planting designer and author. His award-winning gardens have been featured in *The New York Times, Better Homes and Gardens, Martha Stewart Living, Fine Gardening,* and *Garden Design,* as well as numerous television, radio, and digital media appearances.

In his multidisciplinary practice, he explores the intersections of people, plants, and place through ecological, site-specific design and art. He specializes in creating diverse and dynamic gardens that reimagine places for consilient encounters with the natural world. The studio supports other entrepreneurial projects, including The Public Horticulture Company, an emerging ecological landscape firm, and the New Naturalism Academy, a virtual school for enthusiastic designers and gardeners.

Kelly travels widely to explore and study plants in nature. He lives and works at Three Oaks Garden in Des Moines, Iowa.

Photo credit: Austin Hyler Day

Index

A

Abronia villosa (desert sand verbena), *36*

abundance, defined, 188

Acer negundo (box elder), *158*

Acer saccharinum (silver maple), *158*

adaptive management cycle, 49

aeration, 37

    See also soil

aesthetics, 102, 108

Agastache foeniculum (anise hyssop), *82–83*

alder (*Alnus*), 71

allelopathic species, 94

Alnus (alder), 71

Alypia octomaculata (eight-spotted forester), *59*

Amphiachyris dracunculoides (prairie broomweed), 53

Amsonia hubrichtii (threadleaf bluestar), *169*

anise hyssop (*Agastache foeniculum*), *82–83*

annual fleabane (*Erigeron annuus*), *151*

Apis mellifera mellifera (dark European honeybee), 154

apomixis, 89

arborvitae (*Thuja occidentalis*), *115*

arid lands, 170

    management and stewardship, 175

    planting, 171–174

    site conditions, 170–171

asexual seed formation, 89

Asplenium rhizophyllum (walking fern), 86

B

Bad Hair Day switchgrass (*Panicum* 'Bad Hair Day'), *106–107*

Bailey Nursery Display Garden, *108*, *131*

Barbican Centre, 99–101, *163*

bare ground, 68

bareroot planting, 146

Berry, Wendell, 118

Betula (birch), 71

Betula populifolia (gray birch), *29*

Bicknell's sedge (*Carex bicknellii*), *138–139*

biennial gaura (*Oenothera gaura*), 109

big bluestem (*Andropogon gerardii*), *124–125*

bigtooth aspen (*Populus grandidentata*), *159*

biodiversity, 61

    following a disturbance, 30

bioregions, defined, 188

birch (*Betula*), 71

black walnut (*Juglans nigra*), 94

Blank Performing Arts Center, *144–145*

bloom time, 80

blue grama (*Bouteloua gracilis*), 134, *135*

bonsai, and resilience, 48

bottlebrush grass (*Elymus hystrix*), *138–139*

Bouteloua (blue grama), 134

Bouteloua gracilis (blue grama), *135*

Bouteloua gracilis 'Honeycomb' (Honeycomb blue grama grass), *167*

box elder (*Acer negundo*), *158*

C

California poppy (*Eschscholzia californica*), *174*

Callirhoe involucrata (purple poppy mallow), 80

Canada goldenrod, 151

Canadian burnet (*Sanguisorba canadensis*), 80

Capitol Reef National Park, 58

carbon-sequestering plants, 47

carbon-to-nitrogen (C:N) ratio imbalance, 87

Dream of Beauty aromatic aster (*Symphyotrichum oblongifolium* 'Dream of Beauty'), *78–79*

Dunnett, Nigel, planting design, *49, 100–101, 163*

dynamism, 56

E

Echinacea paradoxa (yellow coneflower), 90

Echinacea purpurea (purple coneflower), 90

Echinacea simulate (Ozarks coneflower), 90

Echinocereus engelmannii (strawberry hedgehog cactus), *174*

ecological gardening, vs. organic gardening, 25

ecoregions, defined, 188

ecotypes, defined, 188

editing the garden, 134–135

eight-spotted forester (*Alypia octomaculata*), *59*

Elymus hystrix (bottlebrush grass), *138–139*

emergence, 52

environmental filtering, 61

Epping, Jeff, planting design, *165*

Eragrostis spectabilis (purple lovegrass), *169*

Erigeron annuus (annual fleabane), *151*

erosion, 36

See also soil

Eryngium leavenworthii (Leavenworth's eryngo), *149*

Eschscholzia californica (California poppy), *174*

Eschscholzia minutiflora (pygmy poppy), *74–75*

Euphorbia corollata (flowering spurge), 110–111

evenness, 123

defined, 188

experience, 102

F

Farnsworth's jewelflower (*Streptanthus farnsworthianus*), *42–43*

fertilizers, 94–95

Finite and Infinite Games (Carse), 16

finite games, 16

Fischer, Bryan, planting design, *143*

floral traits, 126

flow, 10, 137

See also nutrients; recycling; reducing consumption; reusing; water flow

flowering spurge (*Euphorbia corollata*), 110–111

fluctuations, 141

foil, 114, *115*

See also structure

forb cover and richness, 68–69

forbs, defined, 188

forests, 156

management and stewardship, 162–163

planting, 158–161

site conditions, 156–158

found objects, 147

frost aster (*Symphyotrichum ericoides*), *78–79*

frost aster (*Symphyotrichum pilosum*), *134*

G

gardening, vs. planting, 11

gardens

defining, 8–9, 138

history, 9

The Gardens on Spring Creek, *143*

Undaunted Garden, *180*

generalist, 56, 86

defined, 188

genotypes, defined, 188

Gerritsen, Henk, 118

Geum macrophyllum (yellow avens), *98–99*

glaciated soil, 156

Glaucium, *72–73*

Glenn, Joshua, 147